TABLEWARE IN CLAY
FROM STUDIO AND WORKSHOP

TABLEWARE IN CLAY FROM STUDIO AND WORKSHOP

Karen Ann Wood

The Crowood Press

First published in 1999 by
The Crowood Press Ltd
Ramsbury, Marlborough
Wiltshire SN8 2HR

British Library Cataloguing-in-Publication Data
A catalogue record for this book is available from the
British Library.

ISBN 1 86126 198 5

Photograph previous page: *A Modern Banquet*.
Stoneware dishes by Sandy Brown.

Dedication
This work is dedicated to Harry who has suffered
and supported, and to Diana and Brenda whose
judgement in matters of clay I trust implicitly.

Typefaces used: text and headings, ITC Giovanni;
chapter headings, ITC Tiepolo.

Typeset and designed by
D & N Publishing
Membury Business Park, Lambourn Woodlands
Hungerford, Berkshire.

Printed and bound in China.

Acknowledgements
I wish to thank most sincerely the following: Alison
Cowling of the Northampton Museum and Art
Gallery, Dr Alan Tyler of the Bromley Museum, Gary
Atkins of Kensington Church Street, Alexandra
Bellamy of Christie's Twentieth Century Studio
Pottery, Camilla Young of Christie's Images, Beverley
Nenk and Derek Lowe of the British Museum, Oona
Wills of The Museum of London and Martin Durrant
of the Victoria and Albert Museum, Gaye Blake
Roberts of the Wedgwood Museum and Penni
Wood, whose precision was invaluable. Grateful
thanks also to all those contributors who gave so
very generously that they made the book possible
and to Hilary who, with great patience, tried to show
me how to edit.

Photographic Acknowledgements
Grateful thanks to the following individuals and
institutions that supplied photographs for the pages
indicated: Ashmolean Museum, Oxford 26; Gary
Atkins 41 (b), 44, 46, 48, 54, 147; Steven Brayne 123,
187; British Museum, London 28–31, 34; Geoffrey
Carr 152 (t), 155; Christie's Images 38–40, 49 (t), 53,
58 (b); Christie's, South Kensington 69, 70 (l and r),
72 (t and b), 74; Lindsay Dack 146 (b), 174–7;
Gallery of Art and Design, NC State 6 (photo Jackson
Smith); Lu Jeffrey 84, 126; Peter Lee 108 (t), 132 (t),
145 (b); Phil Martin 116 (t), 135 (b), 154 (b); David
McArther 102 (b); Tracey Montgomery 176–78;
Graham Murrell 20 (t), 144, 167 (b), 168; Museum
of London 36 (b), 43, 49 (b), 52; Northampton
Museum and Art Gallery 36 (t), 41 (t), 42; John
Polak 134 (t), 153 (b); Neil Richards 166, 184;
Paulina Rook 162; Pierre Soissons 117 (t), 135 (t);
Mike Vandervord 8, 10, 11 (t), 12 (t), 17 (t), 18, 19,
21 (b), 51, 57, 58 (t), 63, 86 (b), 105 (t), 111 (t),
119 (b), 136 (t), 148 (b); Victoria and Albert
Museum, Trustees of 67; Wedgwood Museum 59, 60.
(t) indicates top, (b) bottom, (l) left and (r) right.

Contents

*W*ater-jug, 1998, wood-fired salt-glaze. Mark Hewitt, North Carolina, USA. The potter says: 'Good pots speak a language of their own with a vocabulary as expressive, rich and sophisticated as any other art form. The fact that you can use pots simply adds to their beauty; it certainly does not detract'.

Introduction: Fabric and Firing

Nomenclature

Tableware of fired clay has not always been in general use, nor will it always be in the future. The last few centuries have seen the phenomenal flowering of an industry that fitted a particular requirement. As other materials waned in popularity or became scarce – and therefore expensive – so pottery literally swelled to fill the gap, until we find it difficult to imagine our daily bread on stone or metal plates, in wooden bowls or horn cups. Because this growth was erratic, developing at different times, growing for different reasons, in a variety of places, the words associated with fired clay are unscientific and confusing.

'Pottery', for example, comes from Anglo-Saxon and means fired clay. 'Ceramic' comes from Greek via German and means fired clay. 'Terracotta' comes from Latin via Italian and means fired clay. Strictly speaking all three are interchangeable: the pot that holds petunias in the garden in the summer is pottery, ceramic or terracotta.

Yet terracotta has come to mean the orange-red colour taken on by some fired clays and paint pigments. It has also become synonymous with 'unglazed', though there is no real reason why it should have done so. Ceramic is used to describe the scientific, technical and industrial aspects of clay, yet at the same time has been taken on by artists. Pottery now conjures up pictures of rather cumbersome kitchenware. 'China', though it means no more than pots from that country, has taken on the classier connotation of 'best (white) tableware on the dresser'. A particular type of white glazed ware, often painted with bright colours, might be called 'tin-glaze' in some places, and maiolica, delft or faience in others – the last three names being geographical although the process actually originated in the Middle East.

Though the wares so made are not used for food in the west, *raku* comes from a Japanese ceremony to do with tea, the significance of which is incomprehensible here except to a handful of Oriental scholars. Yet the term is now highly descriptive of a whole range of procedures and results, and is commonly seen in galleries where studio pottery is sold.

Perhaps all this confusion of nomenclature helps retain some of the mystery of what has become an intensely factory-based industry where the needs of millions are catered for with efficiency and cost-effectiveness. Whatever the cause, some explanations are required before the mysteries of hand-produced tableware from studio and workshop, the art or craft that has grown as an alternative to mass production can be appreciated. It is, after all, a fact that both lines sprang from the same beginnings and borrow from each other not just terms but also techniques, though the gap between the two is certain to widen in the future as computer-aided production in factories increases.

The basic material of the craft could provide a basis for simple categorization of different sorts of pots, but clays, even within the same locality, vary to a degree that makes this impracticable. Firing temperature is the usual first line of description, because actual numbers, scientific and unvarying can be applied.

Earthenware

The Firing Temperature

Food has a certain temperature range within which it is cooked. This is dictated by the boiling points of liquids, and though time, heat applied and fuel may vary, the range of the temperatures used remains fairly constant. A normal oven has a top temperature of about 260°C, the heat required to bake a pizza. The same is roughly true of clays. Earthenware describes those pots fired, or baked, somewhere in the range 700–1180°C. Above 700°C,

*P*ickle dish, Sidney Tustin, Winchcombe Pottery, 1930s. This is made of a red earthenware clay, which shows dark brown through the clear lead glaze. The decoration is 'trailed'. Now a slip-trailer is made of rubber or plastic, but potters used to use a cow horn with a quill poked through the small end.

most clays will change to a state of hardness where the shape will not be altered by exposure to water though seepage may occur. This state is irreversible. Another definition of earthenware is that it is fired fabric that has the ability to absorb 5 per cent of its own weight as moisture.

Given clay and fuel, earthenware pots are simple for rural economies to produce. Both these commodities were once in plentiful supply over almost all of Britain. Some earthenware clays, for example those found throughout Staffordshire, fire to a red or

J ug, Huw Phillips, Gladstone Pottery, 1998. Red earthenware with clear lead safe glaze and white slip.

orange colour because of the high iron content. Others, say round Oxford or in Kent, are pale buff to yellowish. Gardeners will recognize the texture and colour of their own local clay seam, the turgid, dense layer that can ruin the drainage of even the best garden beds by stubbornly resisting any attempt by water to escape.

Where the clay is revealed, either round a footring or across the whole base of the pot, fired earthenwares range in colour from white (a recent innovation), to buff or yellowish, to pink, orange, terracotta or dark maroon. If these clays are fired higher than 1200°C (or less depending on the composition) they are inclined to 'bloat', that is, blister-like swellings appear in the fabric. The clay may become very dark and brittle and will no longer absorb any moisture.

Earthenware Glazes

For the making of tableware, earthenware pots are traditionally glazed with one of two sorts of glaze, both of which cover the pot with a hygienic, smooth, moisture-retaining surface suitable for food use. As we will see later, other cultures and societies are or were not so demanding, but it is likely now that only a dedicated collector or pot junkie would knowingly eat from unglazed, lumpy or pitted surfaces.

LEAD GLAZE

The first material that fulfils the glaze requirement for earthenware pots is lead, one of the most useful glaze or glass metals and one with an ancient and venerable history in spite of its more recent bad press.

Lead melts at just the right temperature for earthenware clays and is tolerant to variation – that is, it will make a glaze at 960°C and it will, with some additions, make a glaze at 1200°C.

*J*ug, Ewenny
Pottery, South
Wales, 1930s.
Lead-glazed red
earthenware, fired
to 1080°C in a
coal-fired kiln. The
glaze covers white
slip and the green
in the splashed
decoration is
copper oxide.

*E*wenny jug
close-up. The glaze
was applied in
several layers to give
a thick, rich effect.

*B*ase of an Ewenny
jug. The iron
containing lead glaze
has 'run' into pools at
the base of the pot. So
that it would not stick
to the kiln shelf it was
fired on a three-
pronged 'stilt', which
could be knocked
away after firing. The
pale body was not
local to South Wales,
but imported from
Devon.

In medieval England, lead powder was dusted onto the surface of raw pots, that is pots that had not been fired at all. Often this 'galena' glaze was only used on the outside shoulder since everyone was perfectly accustomed to the unglazed insides to jugs and bowls and had means of coping with the porosity that we, in this highly technical age, have forgotten. The shine this lead gave to the pots made them more like the metal, silver, pewter or bronze vessels used as food servers by the wealthy. The eventual use of the lead on the insides of vessels made them much easier to clean, stronger, longer lasting and hence more valuable.

Lead with the addition of some flint to prevent the glaze running straight off the pot provides a perfect covering for earthenware. It gives a smooth, bright finish, which on a white or pale background shows beautiful colour reactions with the metal colouring oxides: bright green with copper, as in the spectacular pots from the south of France or medieval English jugs, a wonderful rich yellow with some of the iron oxides or a deep, treacle or purplish brown with manganese. To obtain the white or cream background required to show off bright colours, potters whose clay supply was red or dark often painted or dipped pots into a pale clay from another area or clay seam, suspended in water. This is called slip.

Varied colouring possibilities were then made available by pouring and melding further slips of other colours. This technique of slip decorating has a history in Europe as long as lead glazing itself, and reached one of many zeniths in the slipped pots of seventeenth-century England. If a slip-decorated pot is turned over, the demarcation line of the end of the slip can usually be clearly seen with a shiny line below it where there is only glaze.

Sometimes thumb or finger marks are visible in the slip, fingerprints left for all time. This is because the technique of slip decorating – dipping a raw pot into a bucket of thick slip– requires both manual dexterity and perfect timing. It is enormous fun, so students are often introduced to pot making through dipping, pouring, marbling, feathering or trailing different coloured slips. This seems natural in one sense because the tradition is so entrenched in Britain, but in another it seems completely mad since it is a technique that requires such a high level of skill.

RAW LEAD IN USE

In spite of these advantages, lead has some serious defects as a glaze material. One is that in its raw state it is highly poisonous. The potters of the old days dusting raw lead onto their pots day after day stood a good chance of leaving widows to carry on the business. When glaze materials were found to be easier to handle and apply when suspended in water as a glaze slop, the potter would still grind his own lead, adding the sweepings of clay from the workshop floor to aid suspension in the slop and strengthen the melt in the kiln, a double infusion of toxins. If he escaped poisoning by the lead, he stood a good chance of getting silicosis from the silica in the dusty floor sweepings. Regulations now prohibit the use of raw lead compounds in industry and in schools. Effective substitutes, no longer toxic, have been developed by 'fritting' the lead before use and by using other compounds.

Jug, Clive Bowen, Devon, 1997. Traditional-style jug but this time with a lead safe glaze. The clay colour is soft pink where exposed under the pot. The green is copper and the brown is the colour of the clay showing through the white slip.

Mugs, Josie Walter, Derbyshire, 1997. The slip has been painted on to the pots in layers with a large soft brush to give a variegated effect, which allows the clay to show through in places. A line of 'glaze only' can just be seen as a shiny line at the base.

Fritting, which is carried out by companies who specialize in the preparation of materials for potters, is a process whereby materials are heated to temperatures where their physical and chemical composition is altered. They are then cooled and ground to a fine powder for use in glazes. When lead is fritted with silica it is no longer able to release its toxins.

Raw lead can also cause poisoning if it is not well fired and this, not unnaturally, has given the substance an even worse reputation. If the 'melt' has been fully achieved in the kiln and the glaze is completely fused, smooth, uncrazed and bright, then the lead has combined with silica in glaze or body and the leaching of lead into foodstuffs is impossible. Where lead glazes are at all rough to the touch or matt, then strong acids such as vinegar or fruit juices, especially if left to stand, can cause some escape of lead into the food or liquid. This effect is compounded by the use of copper in glaze or decoration.

People all over the world, from the Mediterranean to the Americas to Asia have used lead-glazed cooking pots and tableware for millennia, discovering in the process of using

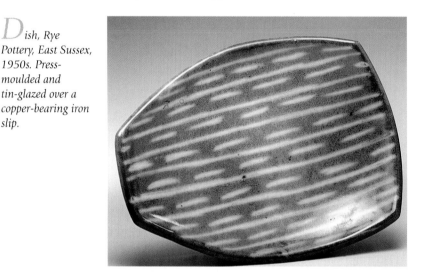

*D*ish, Rye Pottery, East Sussex, 1950s. Pressmoulded and tin-glazed over a copper-bearing iron slip.

them ways to mitigate the chances of lead release. There is no material yet discovered that truly takes its place. The new low-solubility glazes sit as a separate layer on top of slips rather than firing into them to produce lead's soft richness of colour, but the many examples of slipped, clear-glazed pots in this book testify to the modern tableware-potter's inventiveness and artistry in using the more calculated 'safe' glazes required by society.

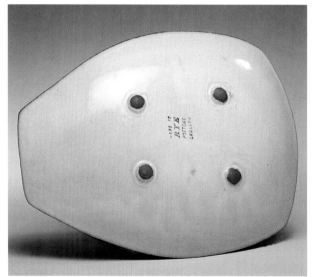

*U*nderside of 1950s Rye dish. The tin glaze is opaque and masks out the darkness of the red clay. The clay is clearly visible where the pot has stood on the kiln shelf.

TIN GLAZE

The other glaze that has traditionally been used in many parts of the world for tableware made at low temperatures is one that contains tin. The particular quality that this material gives to a glaze is a milky white opacity. The colour of the underlying clay is masked with white though a dark firing clay might cause a pinkish tinge. There is no need to use a slip under a tin glaze. The range of available metal oxides – cobalt for

*D*ish, Linda
Arbuckle, Florida,
1997. Contemporary
tin glaze, Maiolica,
Delft or Faience. The
range of colours is
extensive and the
glaze smooth and
well fired. Red
earthenware clay.

blue, copper for green, and iron for browns, yellows and reds – mean that the range of colours possible is large. There are also specialist colour manufacturers, who, by ready-mixing and fritting the oxides, provide the tin-glaze potter with an even greater palette.

Tin has been in use since the Bronze Age, and was mined in Cornwall by the Phoenicians, who called Britain the Cassiterides or 'Tin Islands'. Other European countries also obtained their supplies from the same source. Now potters use tin from large deposits in Bolivia, Malaysia, the Urals and Nigeria; the Cornish mines are all closed. The relative cheapness and availability of tin in the past gave English tin-glazed wares a particularly rich, fat texture, which, for everyday tableware, was often left undecorated.

The height of sophistication for tin glaze came during the Italian Renaissance, when artists embellished the white ground of platters, *albarellos* (drug jars), tiles and fountains with fantastic and beautiful portraits, animals, birds, biblical scenes and coats of arms. The colours used could also include gold and even brighter hues if the fired white pot was painted with gold or enamel colours and put back into the kiln for a third firing, this time not to the 1000°C or more required to melt the glaze, but to about 650°C. This method is used in industry and by studio and workshop potters to extend the range of possible colours.

Both types of earthenware so far described can be fired in a kiln using gas, oil, wood, coal or electricity, but a wood-fired kiln is best for the fascinating but notoriously difficult offshoot of tin glaze – lustre ware, the special preserve of the potters of the Middle East, taken by the Moors to Spain, where it flourished. Chlorides of silver, gold or perhaps platinum are fired into the surface of the glaze, producing a soft, lustrous decoration. In England, the finish was used as a novelty by some factories in the eighteenth and nineteenth centuries. Lustred tableware was revived by an artist potter in the 1960s, Alan Caiger-Smith, but due to the complexities of firing it is not a method to be taken on lightly.

Mugs, Karen Ann Wood, Kent, 1997. These stoneware mugs were fired in an oxidized atmosphere to 1280°C. The clay colour is uniform, which is typical of this type of firing, but the amount of iron in the clay can vary the colour. The opaque white glaze contains tin, but at this firing temperature, lead is no longer effective and other substances, in this case Cornish stone, must be used instead as the main glaze ingredient.

Stoneware

Clays and Firing

Stoneware clays are those that will fire to temperatures of above 1200°C, sometimes as high as 1400°C, without slumping, distorting, or bloating. The word 'stoneware' is an apt one because the closest material in texture, and sometimes colour, to clay fired in this way is stone. Each clay has a different 'best' or optimum temperature, one at which the body is very nearly vitrified but not quite. The fired strength and thermal shock resistance of stoneware is better if there is a small amount of porosity, say up to 2 per cent. A potter friend made perfectly satisfactory pizza platters fired to 1260°C, but a new higher firing glaze caused her to raise the temperature to 1280°C. Every platter subsequently shattered in use and came back, accompanied by an irate purchaser. The problem was that the temperature rise caused the clay to vitrify, that is become absolutely stone-like, with a consequent increase in brittleness and the loss of ability to withstand sudden changes in temperature.

Stoneware was 'discovered' in China or Korea when potters began to understand better the building of kilns that could boost the firing temperature up the extra few hundred degrees. This feat can seem impossible in a too primitive or inefficient kiln, or for that matter in most kilns out of doors in a storm. The colour of the fire at the top temperature of an earthenware kiln is a bright flame red tinged with orange, but by the time the temperature reaches 1300°C in a stoneware-firing kiln the colour is a pale, lemony yellow with white bits round the edges of pots.

The First Stoneware Glaze – Ash

At this temperature wood ash from the firebox of the kiln flies on the strong draught created by the intense heat into the chamber where the pots are placed, then melts over everything, including the pots. This 'glaze' obviously pleased the early kiln firers because they kept using and refining the technique, eventually adding other substances to the ash to vary colour and texture.

Other naturally occurring substances – minerals and rocks – possess the right ingredients to make a glaze at stoneware temperatures. It is not uncommon to find potters

Cooking/ serving dish, Richard Batterham, Dorset. The texture and colour of this ash-glazed dish are typical. The potter has not relied on ash settling randomly on the pots, but has deliberately mixed it into a glaze 'slop'.

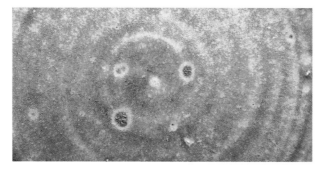

Close-up of the richly varied surface possible with ash glazes.

whose interests lie in developing these for their tableware. The potter I worked with in New Zealand had a wonderfully rich glaze for the insides of bowls. Its recipe read: 'Take eight pounds of mud from the top paddock and mix with water. Sieve and apply thickly.'

Differences between Stoneware and Earthenware

This temperature divide gives other differences beside glaze composition. The colouring oxides tend to be bleached paler as the heat rises, so that stoneware has a more subtle, less predictable colour range. The ebullience of tone possible with say, low-fired tin glaze, is much more difficult, in some cases impossible, to achieve at stoneware temperatures. The most reliable colour throughout the whole range of temperatures is blue, derived from the metal cobalt. Other metals like copper, which gives greens at earthenware, can become fugitive at higher temperatures, in some cases disappearing altogether.

Given that each of the clays has similar working properties (of plasticity, shrinkage and so on) the earthenware kiln will be much more tolerant of unusual or intertwined shapes. A fuddling cup – three mugs or more joined by laced handles, called a 'jolly boy' in Somerset and made as a drinking novelty for social occasions in the eighteenth and nineteenth centuries in tin glaze and in lead glaze – would require very special attention, especially in drying, to be successfully made in stoneware. Shapes for mass production in stoneware have always tended to be fairly simple in design for that reason.

Stoneware for the table has been popular with both potters and collectors since the 1920s, when Bernard Leach and his friend and partner Shoji Hamada revitalized methods, but recent concern over environmental issues has caused many potters to rethink since the energy required to produce stoneware, from whatever source, is disproportionately high.

Reduction Firing

Fuel consumption is even higher if, instead of the atmosphere in the kiln being kept clear and airy throughout the firing ('oxidized'), some of the air supply to the burning fuel is cut off or held back. Since combustion requires oxygen and it is not available as air, the flame robs oxygen from the both clay and glaze, changing them both. This is reduction. The phenomenon first came about because ventilation in kilns was poor. In some places, potters then learnt to manipulate the air supply for special effect. The most startling illustration is the early Egyptian pots, which are half red, half black – half reduced, half oxidized. At high temperatures, reduction can cause copper, which usually makes a range of greens in glaze or decoration, to make the red called *sang-de-boeuf*, while iron oxide, usually associated with earth tones, is capable of a gentle range of greens. Reduction is also used at earthenware temperatures for certain effects or colours, for example for lustres.

*C*asserole, Karen Ann Wood, Kent, 1997. This casserole dish was fired to 1290°C in a gas fired kiln. The glaze is the same all over, but the white part has not been reduced because it was in a part of the kiln that remained well supplied with air. Even the texture of the glaze is different on the lid.

*B*owl, Oldrich Asenbryl, Gwynedd, Wales, 1998. High-fired in a reduction atmosphere, the colours of the bowl soften and change. The mulberry colour is actually copper oxide, and the green is iron. The whole decoration has 'moved' in the kiln in a subtle way with the flow of the glaze.

M*ug, Steve Harrison, London, 1998. This salt-fired mug has a typical texture. The colour comes from an application of cobalt as a slip.*

Salt Firing

A variation on reduced stoneware is the technique whereby, during the latter stages of the firing, common salt (sodium chloride) is thrown or sprayed into the kiln. The sodium thus released combines with the alumina and silica present in the clay to make a thin skin of glaze on the ware. This glaze will be reddish brown or orange if the clay contains much iron oxide and paler grey to white where there is less iron present. Slips of similar composition to those used on earthenware can alter the fired colours of the clay.

B*ase of mug, Steve Harrison. The three little white marks are where the pot stood on alumina wads in the kiln so that it would not stick to the shelf. Shells can also be used for this purpose. Reduction and salting have been light, perhaps because of the pot's position in the kiln.*

Salt glaze originated in Germany, though exactly how it was discovered is a matter for some speculation. It is durable, tough, not at all porous and is resistant to acid attack. Until porcelains were developed in the West, salt glaze was used by chemists and alchemists in the making of crucibles and other laboratory and pharmaceutical utensils. It was also, for the same reason, used extensively for pipes for drainage and sewage once public health schemes were deemed necessary. The Victorian sewage system laid under London is largely salt glazed. Sometimes table and storage pots were made as adjuncts to the construction industry.

C*lose-up of mug, Steve Harrison. Steve uses brass stamps and rollers, which in combination with the salt give a crisp outline to decorative features. He uses paraffin as a releasing agent to free the soft clay from the metal.*

Salt glaze can sometimes be distinguished by its unusual texture – which is mottled, a bit like orange peel – although

the recent interest shown in the method by several proficient studio tableware makers has lead to many subtle variations in texture as well as colour.

Soda Firing

An innovation in achieving the effects of salt glaze without the resultant emission of chlorine gases (which does not endear a salt glaze potter to his neighbours) is to introduce sodium to the kiln in forms other than common salt sodium chloride – for example as baking soda (sodium bicarbonate) or borax (sodium oxide plus boric oxide). These are sprayed under pressure into the kiln at the appropriate time during the firing. This method has all the advantages of salt glazing, and the resultant colours and textures can be equally stunning.

The fabric is strong – longevity is guaranteed barring accidents – and ideal for modern kitchens, where the wear and

Beaker, Patrick Sargent, Switzerland, 1997. This pot bears the unmistakable signs of prolonged firing. The 'glaze' is so well integrated into the body that the two appear to have been born together. In fact the inside of the pot has been glazed, not the outside. White slip has been painted onto the surface when the pot was still soft and this, along with the reduction process, serves to vary texture and colour.

tear of machines and their associated chemicals can wreak havoc on the bone chinas of the last century. Soda firing also has the disadvantages of salt glazing, in spite of being rather kinder to the atmosphere. Kilns used for both types begin to self-destruct right from the first firing, since the salts coat the interior of the kiln, walls, arches and so on; if the glaze so formed is not dealt with, it will not only eat into brickwork, but is likely to melt and drop onto the firing pots.

Base of beaker, Patrick Sargent. If the base had not stood on the alumina wads, this pot would certainly have stuck to the kiln shelf. The long firing time (two days or more), high temperature, reduction, the iron content of the body, clay and wood ash from the fire box have all interacted to glaze the bare clay.

Teapot, Rebecca Harvey, Cambridge, 1997. Soda firing gives the same textures and clean lines to pots as salt firing.

Kilns

Reduced wares can only be satisfactorily fired in a flame-producing kiln using a solid fuel – gas, wood or oil, for example – though some of the most entertaining horror stories about pots and potters come from attempts to 'reduce' the air in an electric kiln by dropping mothballs or silicon carbide pellets through the spyhole. Alan Caiger-Smith relates in *Pots, Potters and Time* a salutary tale of how close he came to having an eye removed by a hot blast of gas hurtling out of the spyhole of his electric kiln when he first attempted to reduce some pots and see what was happening in the kiln at the same time. Salt and soda firings are not possible either, without

Teapot, Chester Nealie, Australia and New Zealand, 1996. The salt kiln has given an unexpected bonus in this rich drop of melted material on the pot. Differences in reduction levels, ash, salt and iron cause the variegated colour and texture.

combustion rather than radiant heat. As electrical elements are improved it is likely that kilns using electricity will become capable of reduction firings, but the fumes given off will still be a limiting factor without extremely efficient ventilation.

The greatest disadvantage/advantage of salt or soda firings is their unpredictability. It was neither here nor there that drainage pipes or tavern jugs had irregular patches of orange-peel interspersed with smooth bits, or were sometimes brown and sometimes a patchy grey or pink. This propensity is as intriguing to the studio potter as it is non-commercial; a factory does not want to say 'sorry, unlikely' when a customer requests an exactly matching piece.

Porcelain

Porcelain is another type of high-fired stoneware. The word describes in most people's minds not a firing temperature,

Interior of a kiln that has been used for high-fired salting, showing the typical glaze skin on the brickwork. The photograph was taken on a university campus, and it is clear that the kiln has suffered at the hands of enthusiastic students. Workshop or studio potters could not afford such disasters, which is not to say that they do not happen. The kiln shelf is now unusable because the accumulated glaze will melt in the next firing and anything on it will be hopelessly stuck.

Bowls, Joanna Constantinidis, Essex, 1996. These porcelain bowls are a fine greenish white. They are thin-walled and translucent.

*P*lace setting,
Bill Brouillard,
Ohio. The intense
colour of this
high-fired porcelain
piece is fostered by
the whiteness of the
body.

but a fragile translucency of fabric and glaze and a preciousness that applies to no other material in the potter's repertoire. Unlike other clays, which can be found in naturally occurring seams or on alluvial flats, porcelain has always been 'made up' in the sense that it is a mix of materials. The Chinese, seeking an elusive whiteness – elusive as most clays contain impurities that prevent it firing white even though it may look pale in the natural state – blended *kao-lin*, a china clay, and *petuntse*, a natural stone (which is called Cornish stone in the UK) and fired the resultant material to stoneware temperatures. This began a tradition that culminated in the superb pots of the Ming Dynasty (fifteenth to sixteenth centuries) – blue and white painted porcelains that made all Europe envious and finally bought clay tableware to the attention of princes.

In China, the clay mix or body was workable by the same means as other clays – wheel throwing, modelling, moulding – but the European versions, when they came, had little plasticity and had to be fired at precisely the right temperature to prevent slumping. Since the material was seen as desirable and valuable it naturally attracted wealthy sponsors who had the power to have factories set up immediately. There has been no tradition of peasant-based or workshop production of porcelain in Europe. It is somewhat ironic that, while in the East porcelain bowls were being banged about in the kitchen or stacked on shelves waiting for crispy noodles, a single specimen in London, Paris or St Petersburg would have been the object of great veneration, to say nothing of expense.

Soft-Paste Porcelain and Bone China

One of the substitutes used by European factories, since they could not discover the secret of true porcelain, was the so-called 'soft paste'. This was fired at low earthenware temperatures. It enjoyed great vogue in the eighteenth century when its capacity to be modelled into fantastic rococo ornament was much appreciated, but it was never as strong or ringing as the true porcelain. The other substitute was 'bone china', developed in England and popular to this day. Bone ash is mixed with china clay and feldspars or Cornish stone to make a body that is short when plastic and so fragile when dry that pieces must be imbedded into a refractory alumina powder or sand for a first, or bisque, firing. This firing is to a stoneware temperature – 1280°C or more and is for translucency. The glaze firing is then quite low, sometimes below 1080°C. A third very low firing is required for the application of certain bright colours (enamels) or perhaps gold rims or banding.

Porcelain in Use

Porcelain itself, the true one, is an extraordinary material, utilized to the full in this century in many industries from electronics to chemistry, space technology to dentistry, paints, cosmetics and the making of paper. Its resistance to acids and heat, its non-conductive properties plus strength under impact and thermal shock-resistance endear it to industry but the qualities most admired by potters are the same as those sought by the Chinese who discovered it – a whiteness that allows great purity of colour, a translucency that allows great play with light and shadow, and a hard, smooth surface capable of being either polished or glazed. Glazes are often thin so that the passage of light is not obscured and can be of great delicacy – pale blues, greens and turquoises in a reducing atmosphere or yellows and creams in a clear or oxidising one. The soft ring of porcelain under knife, fork and spoon combined with the smoothness of surface make it an ideal medium for plates and bowls, cups and saucers but, as with every other type of clay, it does have some drawbacks.

Problems

As a raw material, porcelain is sensuous and smooth. It is also prone to slump and to become flaccid if overworked. This means that the maker must be highly skilled, his movements as crisp as the finished pot. Bentonite, a very plastic clay, is added to increase the plasticity of the clay for forming. Otherwise wheel-throwing, which requires plastic clay, is difficult and edges and handles can split in the same way as 'short' pastry. Makers of porcelain are very careful with the amount and evenness of the water content of work in progress. Pots that are thrown on the wheel in porcelain can be 'turned' or 'trimmed' almost paper thin, but this cannot be overdone because warpage and shrinkage rates are high, and while some movement is charming, a whole kiln-load of bent and twisted porcelain has been known to reduce a normally stoic potter to tears. The glaze firing (1280–1350°C for

Dish, Joanna Howells, Wales, 1998. The water-coloured glaze is typical and is only possible on a pure white body. Only a very small amount of clay is left clear of glaze on the feet. The soft form belies the strength of the fired clay.

porcelain) is likely to produce more 'wasters' or seconds than with any other clay. A well-known sculptor working with porcelain and bone china says that she never knew when she opened the kiln whether there might not just be puddles of glass where she had placed the pots. This is because to get the total vitrification that gives the pots their translucency and strength, they are fired so high that the next stage is, literally, collapse.

The high initial cost of porcelain clay is also a drawback, especially for young potters who have not got the reputation to assure a market at the end of their travail with this most intractable of materials. Both bone china and porcelain have been used as the medium for figurative and sculptural work for many years, but it is only fairly recently that more than a handful of tableware potters have taken the plunge, using the refined qualities of the material to make table pots that are delicate and strong yet in keeping with contemporary taste.

Conclusion

For a variety of reasons, ranging from the artistic to the economic to the practical, potters who specialize in making pots for kitchen or table tend to focus on only one of the above types of ware – at least at any one time. It may be that a particular firing method appeals, or that the maker loves the bright colours of tin glaze, the orange-peel texture of salt glaze or the clean lines of porcelain. Or perhaps the kiln is just too old and tired to get beyond 1200°C. Whatever the method and however innovative the potter, much of the process is rooted in the past and intimately tied up with not just the pots made by our forebears, but also with social and culinary developments that rendered those pots either desirable or necessary or, at the best of times, both. Workshops and studios, in the sense of a few people gathered to make pots from the digging of the clay to the point of sale, have been around for a very long time, much longer than the factories which sprouted up on the back of the Industrial Revolution, and it is their story that will concern us.

I

THE HISTORY OF HANDMADE TABLEWARE

*D*rinking vessel, eleventh century. Red clay with well-fired lead glaze and rhythmical 'throwing rings'. This cheeky mug with its 'grotesque' embellishment was found by T.E. Lawrence (1888–1935) at 7 Cornmarket Street, Oxford, which had been part of a medieval market frontage. Lawrence donated the greater part of his collection of historic pots to the Ashmolean Museum, Oxford.

1 The Humble Beginnings: Neolithic to Tudor

Obviously every old man is not wise; every old pot is not delightful. There is, however, a presence that old pots have.

Michael Simon, potter, Georgia, USA.

Clay Appears at the Table

The art of making fired clay vessels appears to have arrived in Britain about five thousand years ago with a wave of immigration from continental Europe. The immigrants were, if not farmers in the modern sense, at least well enough versed in farming practices to be able to spend a reasonable amount of time in one location. It is probable that survival still depended, as it had for millennia, on the use of wood, stone, reed, bark and animal products, but this new material, clay, pinched into softly baggy containers to resemble the baskets and hide sacs already in use, had a unique usefulness. Seeds, grains, berries, fruits and roots were rendered more digestible, especially out of season, by soaking and slow cooking in the ashes of the fire – a pottage that was both nourishing and warming, and furthermore could be left to look after itself. These simple pots then formed the first 'oven to table' ware.

Inevitably the fabric, decoration and use of these vessels varied regionally according to food availability and preference, and perhaps even ritual or burial practices. In the Orkneys, where Caithness stone splits easily into flat slabs, people fashioned furniture – dressers and beds, tables and sideboards. The round bases on coiled or pinched pots, so suited to uneven floors, were replaced by flat bases. In the more northerly areas, oats or barley were made into cakes and baked flat on a heated stone. Further south, mixed grains were baked under an upturned pot to keep them moister and lighter.

Bowls, jars, small pots that may have contained salt or incense, pots with clay lids or those recessed to take a stone or wooden lid, pots with lugs used to tie down a skin covering,

Peterborough ware pot, c2500 BC. Marks were made in these pots with bird bones and pieces of twisted hemp or cord. The groove under the rim was for tying on a skin or intestine lid. It would also have made a convenient hold for grasping. Sometimes pots like this were put into the rivers with offerings. This one was found in the Thames. It has a deliberate and unhurried look, as though the maker had made many others.

pottery spoons, burial urns containing human remains – these have all been uncovered on Neolithic sites but we cannot know exactly how or with which tableware meals were taken.

In Egypt I once ate breakfast of a porridge of grains of some sort which had been burst by soaking and cooking slowly overnight in milk. This is the frumenty eaten by our early ancestors, and it was easy to imagine a family group sitting round a large pot of this sustaining gruel, perhaps flavoured with honey or wild fruits or animal bits left over from a kill, before setting out on a day's hunting, gathering or farming.

The Bronze Age

The first pots that seem conclusively to have been for the table, or at least for drinking and feasting, are the beakers of the Bronze Age. These are finely made and elaborately decorated, mostly tall, waisted and open-mouthed – a sure invitation to drink. For the first time, they seem to have belonged to individuals. The status and strength of the people may have been indicated by the quality of the vessel with which he or she was buried. The remains of a lime flower- and meadowsweet-flavoured mead (a drink made from fermented honey) have been found in beakers in Scotland. It has been speculated that this drink may have been the beginnings of Britain's love of alcohol. It may even be that the intricate marks of stripes and chevrons that decorate these fine pots were impressed with hemp or cannabis. If that was incorporated into the mead, the resulting cocktail could have been well worth a special pot and a special party as well.

The Iron Age

The Iron Age, which roughly lead up to the millennium, bought increasing social organization to the people of the British Isles, in part stimulated by the increasing efficiency of weapons in use. Families or tribes lived together in fortified hilltop towns, often with well-defined communal cooking, storage and public areas. Pots became increasingly differentiated in size and shape and in the care with which they were manufactured. In some places, pottery seems to have gone into purposeful production. The ware from the Lizard in Cornwall, naturally tempered with a coarse igneous rock, was evidently particularly successful as the pots travelled many kilometres north and east. One has even been excavated as far away as Calais.

Beaker. These were made over wide areas of Europe for a period of a thousand years 2700–1700 BC. The decorations are fastidious and considered, often much more intricate than this elegant version.

By the first century BC, a coinage had been introduced and the potter's wheel arrived at last after a long journey begun two thousand years earlier in the Middle East through Europe and the kingdom of Gaul to the east coast of England. This 'slow wheel' may have been no more than a piece of wood on a spindle stuck into a cylindrical hunk of rock, where one hand turned the table so formed while the other manipulated the clay. The technique required skill, so that pottery, from being a homestead craft, moved into the workshop in places where there was a labour force surplus to the requirements of day-to-day food production. Shapes became more sinuous and varied, with many small bowls, platters and drinking cups as well as large storage vessels and more elegant pedestal forms.

The rich Belgic (or Celtic) chieftains of the time were buried with their most precious possessions – of gold, silver, bronze, iron and amber as well as fine pottery and amphorae containing the dregs of wine from the Mediterranean, which came by way of Greek traders from a colony in Marseille. Drinking and feasting were obviously a very important part of life.

Celts of Gaul and Britain took their wine undiluted, a practice unheard of in Greece and Rome, where large pots were used especially for the purpose of mixing wine with water. 'And since they partake of this drink without moderation by reason of their craving for it they fall into a stupor or state of madness', wrote Diodorus Siculus in the first century BC.

Foods were now better preserved in the form of butter, cheese, bacon and dried or salted fish. The gradual consumption of such preserved foods during the winter months may have encouraged the use of vessels for specific table use, as well as necessitating a variety of storage vessels.

The Romans in Britain

The Roman invasion of Britain began in the middle of the first century AD. Much evidence, both documentary and archaeological, exists to give a relatively clear picture of the everyday life of these remarkable people. No sooner had the first battalions landed than in came the Roman merchants and army contractors to secure the stores to service the military machine. The stimulus to local production involved the native Britons even if it did not assimilate them. Native workshops making clay pots tempered with crushed flint or shells found themselves updated, rationalized and inundated with orders.

Where a suitable workforce or wares could not be found, the Roman army set up its own potteries, using artisans from among its own ranks or bought in from other colonies, especially Gaul. Workshops, some of them so big that they could be described as industrial complexes, were to be found at one time or another around all the major towns: Oxford, Chichester, Colchester, Doncaster, Lincoln, Peterborough, Winchester, Canterbury and St Albans. Much of the work carried out was for the construction industry – tiles, bricks and pipes for water and waste – but a great deal was also for the kitchen and tableware, which the Romans were accustomed to and demanded.

For the native Britons, food was regional and seasonal, as were their clay pots and pans. To the socially sophisticated and well-educated invaders, both were as subject to fickle fashion as they are now, so that this account, covering as it does a four hundred-year period, must of necessity be generalized. Styles changed often and were different for country and town, consul and slave.

First and foremost, the Romans were excellent and versatile farmers. They introduced and grew successfully many new foods such as walnuts, sweet chestnuts, mulberries, lettuces, sage, rosemary, garlic, parsley, borage and radishes. Pigs were for the first time penned and fattened for the table. Pheasants, peacocks, guinea fowl and fallow deer were bought into the country and, showing great adaptability, the Romans improved the native cattle stock though beef was not common in Rome. Bees were kept and grapes were grown for wine. Shellfish, especially oysters, were raced around the country on the new roads. What the wealthy could not have grown here they imported. Dates, pine nuts, olive oil and olives were among the imports from the Mediterranean. Pepper, beloved by Roman diners, as well as ginger and cinnamon, came by caravan and ship from further afield. Liquamen, a sauce concocted of various fish – mullet, sprats and anchovies plus the entrails of

*R*omano-British beaker, from about AD 150. The indented sides of this drinking goblet mark it as coming from Britain or Gaul since this technique was not used elsewhere. This one is from the New Forest in Hampshire.

larger species – was dried, salted then packed into terracotta amphorae to be shipped to the extremities of the empire. Many such amphorae have been excavated along Hadrian's Wall. One pot from a warehouse in Pudding Lane in London bears the clear inscription 'Lucius Tettius Africanus supplies the finest fish sauce from Antibe'. A flavour to assuage even the worst case of homesickness.

The Roman diners preferred their sauces to be served separately from roasted meat or fish, so the plethora of small bowls and flattish saucers in use could have contained liquamen alone or elaborate confections of dried fruits with grated bread, vinegar, minced onion, garlic and herbs, even blood or entrails. It was believed that digestion was aided by the prone position, so diners half lay or lolled on couches arranged on three sides of the table and were served by slave or servant from the fourth side. Dishes were pushed across the table, which may account for their generally sturdy though highly refined forms.

*R*oman bowl, second or third century AD. Some of this red polished Samian ware was produced in Britain, but this very simple and usable bowl possibly came from Gaul, though it was found in England. The crispness of the changes of direction is a delight.

Spoons, sometimes with a pick at one end for shellfish, were in use for the often soft foods, though hands were the main utensil and handwashing was frequent. Large napkins were provided. Bones, pips, cores and other waste were dropped onto the floor. A child in an Italian children's story explains that that is why the floor mosaics in Roman *triclinia* or dining rooms are distinguished by having patterns of fish bones, fruit cores or other detritus incorporated in their patterning.

The kitchen was well equipped, with a brick hearth to one side straddled by iron bars and with an oven set into one side. In better-off kitchens, there was a range of saucepans, baking dishes and frying pans in bronze or copper, but all cooks had a variety of locally made cooking pots that were cheap and could be thrown away when they could no longer be cleaned properly.

One of the earthenware dishes that was taken to the table was a *patina*, a casserole without a lid, perhaps containing a dish of pounded boiled brains mixed with milk, eggs and plenty of seasoning and herbs, lightly cooked on the brazier and sprinkled with more herbs before being taken to the table. The brains were pounded in a *mortarium* – a thick grit-lined bowl with a pouring spout, of which examples have been found on kitchen sites throughout the Roman Empire, copied from the Greeks who also used them widely. From a potter's point of view, though, the Roman craftsmen were the supreme makers. There are many examples in museum collections, but a favourite is in the British Museum and bears the bold stamp Sereverus over the rim.

We will come across other examples of potters making a particular form or shape because it fitted its purpose exactly. The maker has no doubt of his brief and the result is simple, sure and honest. Altogether, from flagon to drinking cup, *mortaria* to ornate Samian bowl, the tableware products of the time of the occupation reflect a social sophistication, a delight in the pleasures of the table and a delicacy not seen in Britain again for centuries.

The End of Rome in Britain

During the occupation, the old traditions of the household making of clay pots continued among people whose lives were hardly touched by this military and agricultural machine. This was fortunate since in the space of hardly a hundred years marauding bands of Picts, Irishmen, Saxons and Danes, coupled with the withdrawal of Roman troops to other parts of the troubled empire, meant that the 'blip' that had been Rome in Britain disappeared. The pot workshops had used the fast wheel, plaster for mould making, kilns, both single and multi-flued of various sizes, slips for trailing, lead glazes and rich terra-sigillata slips to render wares impervious to liquids. All that technology, along with its products, tablewares, water pipes, bricks, tiles and craftsmen, went with the Roman troops. The remaining population sometimes forcibly, sometimes peaceably, settled with the newcomers into the period from about the sixth century to the Norman Conquest, which is known as Anglo-Saxon age.

The Anglo-Saxons

These were a simpler people altogether than their predecessors. They enjoyed ale drinking greatly and it is through them that Britain's roadways became peppered with ale houses and taverns, though mead continued to be the drink of both Celtic and Saxon aristocracy. A favourite drinking vessel was a horn, which could not be set down until it was drained. The use of domestic ceramics was restricted to those who could afford the luxury of imported Mediterranean wares, which were by this time decorated with Christian symbols such as fish or crosses. Locally produced pots were once more homestead made, fired in clamped or earth-covered bonfires, and round-bottomed owing to the return of open-hearth cookery.

Unless pepper and other spices could be imported (and trading through the sea ports of the south and east coasts never fully ceased), plain food became standardized for most of the population – coarse breads, cheese, pork, fresh or smoked or brined as bacon, and the food that had never been replaced as a staple and was not to be dislodged until after the Tudors, pottage. Wood, horn, metal and leather were the preferred materials for tableware. The better-made pots, many of them used as funerary urns, are not without their own charm. They are fatly rounded at the bottom, narrow-necked, with pushed-out bosses, incised lines and dots and, later, stamped decorations.

Church Influence

It was the flourishing of the church in the sixth century and the subsequent urban developments around the great monastery complexes that gave impetus to the regrowth of much art and industry, including that of the potter. Workers from the Rhineland bought back not only the wheel but the secrets of covered kiln firing, and, long after its introduction in other parts of Europe, the practice of dusting the pots with galena, a lead ore. From East Anglia, then from Stamford in Lincolnshire (which made the finest of these pots) a 'ripple' spread through the country, taking the kiln and wheel with it, though the ripple was by no means even and many isolated parts of Celtic Britain remained without ceramics.

Into the Middle Ages

The centuries following the Norman invasion saw widespread advances in many fields as urban populations increased. Potteries sprang up to take advantage of an increasing demand for domestic wares – jugs, cooking pots, aquamaniles for washing hands at table, pipkins, skillets, bowls and pancheons.

Most pots were undecorated but in some places, where a potter could command a higher price for his goods, the decorations ran riot. And it was on the pitchers, made in huge quantities in some areas, that attention was lavished. Jugs were incised, impressed, festooned with scales or pads of clay, adorned with faces or animal heads, painted and scrolled with slips, glazed green with rich copper/lead mixtures or yellows and oranges over clays with greater or lesser iron content. The potters of Rye in East Sussex swathed their jugs with modelled knights in armour and hunting scenes. Much of the decoration is said to have been derived from foreign imports, but 'foreign' is hardly an apt description, since during this time parts of France were much more closely related to England than were, say, Wales or the north west. Edward I (1272–1307) married first Eleanor of Castile, then Margaret of France. Henry II married Eleanor of Aquitaine. The parts of France that he did not own, she did. Henry VI was crowned King of France in Paris in 1431, though to be fair there was another French King at the time. French was the language of the courts and aristocracy. Cross-channel connections were surely too close for jugs from, for example, Rouen to be called imports.

Pottery was rarely used as tableware except in the most humble households. The wealthy were served meals on large platters of gold, silver, pewter or bronze. These 'messes' were shared by diners using fingers or spoons. 'Trenchers' of stale bread were used for individual servings: 'He is a valiant trencher-man' from *Much Ado About Nothing* by William Shakespeare (1598) had nothing to do with fighting ability or a pit in the ground.

Food was often, like the pitchers, rather on the riotous side, wonderful mixtures of sweet and savoury, highly coloured with saffron or sandalwood, parsley juice or cooked blood, highly flavoured with pepper, cinnamon, ginger, verjuice (a crab-apple vinegar), honey or raisins.

Mediaeval pitchers, thirteenth and fourteenth centuries. The one on the left, with its very sure form, is later than the other two. All are decorated with care and are too elaborate for the dairy, where plain coarseware sufficed. The handles really are for business – nothing slack or flabby about them.

Dame Alice's Purchases

Dame Alice de Bryene was the Lady of a baronial household outside Colchester. Her household accounts for the year 1413 give a fascinating glimpse into the day-to-day life of the sort of feudal household that was in existence over much of the land. Sugar had been brought back by Crusaders returning from the Middle East. Dame Alice purchased only four ounces of this precious commodity, which would have been locked away in a special box. It cost her five pence. At the same time she bought two pounds of ginger for forty pence, eleven pints of honey for nineteen pence, one pound of almonds for two and one half pence (easy to see why they were so widely used) and one pound of saffron for the huge sum of thirteen shillings or one hundred and fifty six pence. These purchases then flavoured the staple meat for midday dinners, which Dame Alice ate with her household and visitors in the Great Hall. On Fast Days in winter the spices would have been especially welcome to modify the strong taste of stockfish, so called because it had to be beaten severely with a stock before soaking and boiling. Ale, brewed on the premises, and imported wines were the main drinks. Thirty-two cups were bought for twenty-four pence 'against the nativity of our Lord'. The material of these cups is not specified. They were certainly of wood, perhaps ash, since anything other is named. In fact four pans to catch dripping were purchased along with a 'streynour' (colander). These are described as 'earthen' and the lot cost eight pence.

The century leading up to Dame Alice's steward's careful accounting had been characterized by wars, famines and plagues. The Black Death of 1348 alone saw off one-third of the population. The century after was characterized by civil unrest interspersed with progress in preparation for change. Henry VII's (1485–1509) interests lay in developing foreign trade and in increasing the takings from his crown estates – in short the making of money rather than war. This in turn lead to an increase in spending power, not only of the powerful nobles and merchant guilds, but also by extension more modest establishments. William Caxton was able to set up his first printing press in the shadow of Westminster Cathedral late in the fifteenth century. This had long-term implications for the dissemination of information of every sort, including household management, cookery, alchemy, the sciences, and details of what the French, Germans and Dutch were doing in all those disciplines.

The First Stoneware

What the potters of the Rhineland and Westerwald were doing had a more visual and tactile impact. From the mid-thirteenth century, a lucrative trade in tavern wares had grown up through the powerful middlemen of the age, the Hanseatic League merchants. They bought to the south and east a vast number of the so-called Bellarmine or D'alva flagons along with globular drinking mugs, made of a tough stone-like fabric, not glazed at first but later with a thinnish grey or pale sheen to them. These vessels were both impervious to liquids and – even better – resistant to acid attack. This made them of particular use to metallurgy and alchemy as crucibles and drug jars but the greater volume was used in taverns and ale houses, often stamped specially with the symbol of the tavern, say a cock or a lion, or with the stamped initials of the tavern's host. The custom was for the pot of ale to be carried home full to be returned at a later date, though the number of signed specimens found in excavations of private dwelling houses would indicate that they often were not returned.

It is a subject for great speculation as to why this new fabric was not manufactured in England. The solution probably lies in the fact that the kiln technology was not available and that indigenous potters simply could not, or did not, realize that they should fire to considerably higher temperatures.

The greatest effect of the use of the salt glaze Rhenish wares was to popularize the idea that drinking from pottery was as good an option as using wood or pitch-lined leather.

Tudor Times

Many potteries flourished during the growth periods of the sixteenth century, making drinking vessels of one sort or another, which is why potters often came to be called cuppers. Since large orders were forthcoming, from the colleges in Oxford, the rich Guilds of London, the great houses and hunting lodges of the high-spending courts of the late Tudors and early Stuarts, or, before the dissolution of 1548, the monasteries, loose conglomerates of potters were formed. One of these, located on the Hampshire-Surrey border, made a fine range of 'tudor-green' or 'border' ware, using a fairly close-textured pale buff clay covered with a lead and copper glaze. Others, in the Midlands, made either 'black-wares' of well-fired dark clay under an iron and manganese bearing glaze, or 'yellow-wares', where the glaze was made honey-coloured by the addition of small amounts of iron. The technique for the firing of these very fine vessels, some of the most satisfying ever to have

Condiment dish and porringer, fifteenth/sixteenth centuries. The condiment dish is a very deliberate table piece and was probably used for the sort of sweet/sour pickles we would recognise now. The porringer was used for pottage, eaten as a staple all over the country. It is from either Staffordshire or Derbyshire. The handle is quite delicate and the decoration rhythmically executed in yellow and dark brown slips.

been made, not just in this country but in the world, may have indeed come from abroad, but the restraint in decoration and the purposeful nature of the forms speak of an intimate acquaintance with local conditions.

Some of these drinking mugs were large and have two or more handles for drink sharing – a habit the French deplored. Some are made for fun, like the puzzle-jugs, where an unwary imbiber could well find his measure of ale poured down his doublet – great exercise for an ingenious potter. The range of beverages had grown. There were, in addition to the widespread ales, milk products, buttermilk and whey, cider and perry, a new beer brewed with hops, buttered ales served hot, possets and caudles, wines from France and sack or sherry from Spain, meads still in country areas and methleglin in Wales. And the potters catered for all of these. By the reign of James I (1603–25) clay drinking pots were firmly established as competitive in the markets and sold alongside coarsewares – pancheons for the dairy, baking-dishes, butter pots, brew pots, and chamber pots. The range of specialized shapes had grown greatly from the preceding centuries. However, further events were to set clay on its way to being the supreme material for general table use, hardly a hundred years later.

Double-handled tankard, Midlands blackware, fifteenth/sixteenth centuries. The rilled pattern was common on these wares and is an imitation of wood. The pot is very well fired and both fabric and glaze are fine and well prepared. It is likely that an improvement in kiln building accompanied this type of ware.

2 Delft, Stone and Slip

As white as jade,
as thin as paper,
as bright as a mirror,
as sound as a bell.

Old Chinese description of porcelain

Delft – A Porcelain Substitute

In 1498 the Portuguese, indefatigable seekers of the spices Europe craved, and the most enterprising sailors of the time, found a sea route to the East Indies. They were inspired in part by the feat of Christopher Columbus in finding what he mistakenly thought were the Spice Islands several years earlier. Among the many commodities the merchants of the Portuguese fleet traded to the envious rest of Europe were blue and white Ming Dynasty bowls from China, made of a material not known before in the West. We can easily view these bowls now in museums or in the great country castles and houses open to the public, but to see them through sixteenth-century eyes it is better to look at Flemish still-life paintings of the time. Most people had never seen white pots, let alone pots so fine, so pearl-like, so translucent, so softly blue in decoration yet so hard in fabric. Unfortunately only the richest could aspire to own them.

However, a fair substitute was at hand, for the art of making, not porcelain, but common red earthenware into snow-white pots by mixing the lead glaze with tin arrived with Flemish potters after a long journey from the Middle East. This process was variously called maiolica, faience and delft. All refer to the same process. But the last name, delft, was possibly more widespread here in the past and came to mean any white earthenware. Peig Sayers, in the poignant story told by her of life on Great Blasket Island, off the west coast of Ireland, at the end of the nineteenth century is comforted on her marriage and move to her mother-in-law's house by seeing 'a neat lamp hung by the side of the wall and the dresser laden with delf.'

The Tudors and Delft

Henry the Eighth (1509–47) is said to have been so impressed by the 'gallipots' (as the whiteware was called then) he saw on a state visit to Amsterdam that he invited

Still Life with Wild Strawberries, Adriaen de Coorte, active 1683–1707.

the potters to come to England in return for 'good wages and house-room'. Several years later, when the first Elizabeth reigned, two Flemish potters began to make the pots, first in Norwich then in London. Over the next century and a half there were many exchanges of potters between the two countries, the flow regulated by the political situation. At first the forms and decorations were modelled on what was being done in the workshops of the Netherlands, but later, when trade was restricted, potters responded to changes in domestic requirements and a more distinctive English style developed.

Tableware for the Gentry

For the first time since the Romans, pots were made specifically for the tables and the more intimate dining rooms of the well-to-do. Over the following fifty years workshops were set up in Vauxhall, Southwark, Bristol (Brislington), Liverpool, Dublin and Wincanton, producing an array of dishes, platters and plates, mugs, wine flagons, salt pots, porringers (a one- or two-handled small bowl) candlesticks and puzzle-jugs, fuddling cups and tankards, the demand depending on a bewildering array of factors.

In the first place, dining rooms had steadily shrunk. Even Elizabeth I often retired to her 'privy-chamber' to eat while the pomp of the more public meal in the Great Hall proceeded without her and her close courtiers. The dissolution of the monasteries by Henry released land to assist the rise of a newly rich landed class, which was augmented after the setting up of the highly successful East India Company in 1600. There was a general increase in the population anyway, and though many, like the widow in Chaucer's *Nun's Priest's Tale*, lived on a poor diet of an inferior bread, some cheese, bacon (pigs were still kept, even in towns) and sometimes an egg, the number of people with spending power grew.

Delft was a fine substitute for the silver, silver plate and pewter that this stratum of society could not afford, though Samuel Pepys, a high-ranking naval official during and after the time of the Commonwealth (1640–62) still boasted of his silver. This paragraph is well worth the quoting since it shows wonderfully the mood of the country after the devastation of the Great Fire of 1666:

Our enemies, French and Dutch, great, and grow more by our poverty. The Parliament
backward in raising, because jealous of the spending of the money; the City less and
less likely to be built again, everybody settling elsewhere, and nobody encouraged
to trade, a sad vicious negligent court and all sober men fearful of the ruin of the
whole kingdom next year; from which God deliver us! One thing I reckon remarkable
in my own condition is, that I am come to abound in good plate, so as at all
entertainments to be served wholly with silver plates, having two dozen and a half.

The meals eaten by the Pepys household were simpler than they would have been in the
preceding century. He had a dinner with friends in June 1664 of 'a good dish of roast
chicken, pease (pudding), lobsters and strawberries,' though there are mentions of dishes
we may not fancy now, such as a pie of lamprey, a fish much favoured by the court. Two
courses were served, each having at least one meat dish as well as sweet puddings.

New Foods

SUGAR

Sugar was now grown in the West Indies and used increasingly instead of honey, the production of which never recovered from the Dissolution, since the monks were the most
noted apiarists in the land. The part-refined sugar was sold in large cones, from which
lumps were hacked off for use in the kitchen.

*London Delft
caudle cups in blue
and white painted
tin glaze. Caudle
was a warmed ale
drink thickened with
eggs. It might be
taken early in the
day as a morning
draught, or in the
evening in lieu of
supper (C. Anne
Wilson,* Food and
Drink in Britain*).*

*F*lemish
*Still Life, attributed
to P. G. Roestraeten,
c1630–1700.
A Yixing metal-
mounted teapot on
a stone ledge with
eight Chinese export
pieces.*

COFFEE

The first coffee house opened in Oxford in 1650 and others soon followed in London. The price was, and remained, prohibitive and the houses became either gentlemen's clubs, or places of business, as at Lloyds. The French authorities feared that the coffee houses would have an adverse effect, since for the first time in Western European history, social gatherings could be conducted without the participants getting drunk, and sober men could be dangerous. They were right, because in the French case coffee became cheaper once plantations were set up in French colonies, and the coffee houses developed into cafés, those notorious hotbeds of intellectual and revolutionary ideas.

Coffee was introduced early into the American colonies, and it was said that the planning for the Boston Tea Party was carried out in the coffee houses of that city.

TEA

Tea also began its path to becoming a national drink from the tables of the rich, who felt their 'China' cups and saucers precious enough to be depicted with them in portraits of the time. These wares arrived courtesy of the English East India Company traders after

1600. At first each drinker had a little tea set of his own with pot, handleless cup, sugar bowl, teapot for brewing and a salver to stand the pieces on. The first tea houses, such as Lyons, were advertised as being especially for ladies, who had previously been confined in their outings to their own and other ladies' drawing rooms. Delft could be made into the requisite teaware but it was nowhere near as heatproof as 'China' so it was only a matter of time and trade embargoes by the Chinese before another home-grown, if not home-inspired, material was found.

OTHER BEVERAGES

Delft better suited the longer drinks of the day, for example posset, a frothed mixture of wine or ale, milk and eggs, or, newly brought from India and the West Indies – punch. Very handsome bowls were made in tin glaze for this alcohol, fruit juice, sugar and water mixture, which has come to symbolize mixed-sex social drinking in the very nicest way. Some bear inscriptions or good wishes. Some have

Posset pot, blue and white English Delft, late seventeenth century. Posset, a warm milk and wine or ale curdled drink, was poured or sucked from the spout, behind which is a strainer. After New Year in 1659 Mr Pepys took his wife 'it being a great frost, to Lady Jems to eat a sack (sherry) posset'.

Bristol Delftware punchbowl, c1730. The 'squirrel and vine' decoration is meant to be viewed upside down as the pots were stored on shelves that way to keep them clean and ready for use. The squirrel is on the other side of the bowl.

advice for polite company: 'Drink square, Don't sware'. More ominous is 'Drink drink whilst ye have breath, for there is no drinking after death'. The writing is a reminder that the delft potters, or at least the decorators, were literate at a time when this was not generally the case.

Decoration on Delft

Pots were painted in very much the current styles of engravings, silver, and other decorative arts of the day. The Low Countries were no less adept at horticulture then than they are now and a wave of tulip-mania was depicted on some of the early English chargers and plates. This abated as relations with the Dutch worsened. The return of the monarchy after the Commonwealth in 1662 saw many spirited depictions of Charles II and his consort Catherine of Braganza; the latter advanced the cause of tea drinking greatly, even bringing her own 'China' with her into the marriage.

The Chargers

The paintings on delft pots, heavily influenced by the designs on Chinese porcelain at first, varied from the accomplished to the naive to the hopelessly inexpert and funny. English potters had, after all, never been required to use a brush before. But between using the Chinese pots as models and the exchange of potters with the delft workshops in Flanders, where there were apprenticeships and training facilities, they learned. The development of a distinct style can be best seen in the large chargers or platters, which were made and survive in relatively large numbers. In part this may have been because William of Orange (1688–1702), with typical Protestant economy, handed them out to his esteemed citizens as an alternative to silver whenever a gift was called for. Since he was from the Netherlands and at one time ruled both Holland and Britain, and had an eye on trade, this was not surprising. A gift from a monarch was to be treasured by even those least committed to the royals, whether mayor, councillor or squire.

Delft charger c1680. The blue, green and yellow decoration is sponged and painted. Adam and Eve look suitably coy but it is difficult to believe that the painter had ever seen anything resembling a serpent.

The one-person dinner plates have not survived intact in such numbers. One in the Ashmolean Museum reads 'on me to eat both sauce and meat', indicating a new culinary trend. Perhaps the separate 'sawcer' was already being put underneath small teacups.

The coming of the fork in the late seventeenth and early eighteenth centuries helped popularize clay-baked plates since they did not mark like pewter and wood did when

*D*elft plate for a
single serving. The
motto in blue is a
reminder of the
ever-present threat
of plague.

meat was held down and cut up. There was much ridicule meted out to this new utensil and it took a very long time to establish itself in England. Queen Anne (1702–14) was said to continue to use her fingers at meals, though in the preceding century a long fork had been very useful for those dandies whose stiffened neck ruffs rendered them almost incapable of feeding themselves by any other means.

The Rise and Fall of Delft

The delft factories, for by the eighteenth century that is what they were, employed numbers of unskilled labourers, many specialist decorators, throwers, turners and glaze-grinders. They grew in size with their export orders. Much was sent to the New World, especially from Bristol and Liverpool, although a factory in Burlington, New Jersey, produced tin glaze in America using clay imported from England before good clay sources were located.

Inevitably the style and forms of the delft pots changed. Further Chinese influence came to bear when restrictive import practices were lifted, and some of the freshness of the early painting slackened. Delft chipped easily and was relatively soft compared to both porcelain and the improved English earthenware, so by the latter half of the eighteenth century manufactories and workshops were disbanding. By about 1790 they had gone.

*C*entre: Fulham
Pottery stoneware
mug c1680–90.
Right: jug from
Derbyshire, possibly
Chesterfield, c1785.
Left: a Sussex lead-
glazed earthenware
'barm pot'. The mug
was inspired by a
Westerwald
stoneware form and
has counterparts in
Staffordshire lead-
glazed earthenware.

Stoneware

Stoneware and John Dwight (died 1703)

Another type of tableware that would later be wiped out under the onslaught of improved earthenware of Stoke on Trent was that of the early stoneware industry. John Dwight was not the first or only person to make this ware, but his story illustrates vividly the new forces that were abroad in the seventeenth century – those of rationalism, science and changing social patterns.

A MAN OF SCIENCE

Dwight spent his early years just outside Oxford, where his family were freeholders on a smallholding. It seems likely that his father was illiterate, but John went to school in Oxford and thence to university to study 'civil law, Physick a little, but mostly chemistry'. As a young man he worked with Robert Hook, who later moved to London to become City Surveyor,

Professor of Mathematics at Gresham's College and curator of experiments for the Royal Society (where Samuel Pepys witnessed experiments, for example showing that combustion required air and that a man will not die immediately if injected with sheep's blood).

Robert Boyle, under whom both Dwight and Hooke worked, was the 'Father of Chemistry' and one of the greatest scientific investigators of all time. While he worked in Oxford it is almost certain that Dwight would have had access to a newly translated book by the German alchemist, Johann Glauber, called *Philosophical Furnaces*. In it Glauber points out that the crucibles made in Hessia in Germany are better than any others, not because their clays are better or different, but because in this area there is 'no sparing of the burning'. A small fire of turves is not good enough. He also advises mixing clays with fine sand (to provide a flint-rich body); taking great care in the making of vessels because of the 'violent fire'; and introducing some salt into the fire to make the pots more resistant to the attacks of metals. He was obviously not too interested in the aesthetic quality of the wares.

It is not clear whether Dwight himself was a potter, but he employed potters known to have worked in other parts of London in his pottery at Fulham, which was then a small village well outside London. Fairly close copies of Rhineland wares were made – mugs, jugs and tankards in the typical salt glaze colours of brown, grey and pinkish orange – many with tavern or tavern owner's names or symbols on applied medallions of clay. A contemporary account states that potters were making 'a range of ordinary stonewares along with red bastard china ware and a very fine sort of ware inlaid with views like marble, and some finely flowered, not painted, but wrought artificially', perhaps referring to the 'sprigging' in different coloured clays typical of some Fulham products.

There is no evidence that 'China', which Dwight claimed to be able to make, was ever produced, but the many test pieces excavated at the site testify to his unending enquiries, and the finely potted white stoneware, several examples of which are to be found in museum collections, are as pleasing in their elegance and subtlety as the porcelain he was so anxious to make.

DWIGHT'S LEGAL ACTIVITIES

Most of the documentary evidence of John Dwight's activities is of a legal nature. In 1672 he had applied for, and was granted a patent for the making of 'cologne ware, transparent earthenware and china'. Much energy went into protecting this patent as he was determined that no one else should use his secret recipes. He actually sued many potters. Notable among them was James Morley of Nottingham, who was an entrepreneur and businessman rather than a potter and whose 'manufactuary' in Nottingham made the very precise and lustrous salt-glazed stoneware now known as Nottingham Brown. It is a measure of the huge popularity of the new beverages, albeit among the rather well-to-do, that Morley made mostly tea and coffee wares, but distinctive also are the loving cups, double-handled for shared drinking and frequently inscribed or sgraffitoed with the owners' names or special dates. Morley seems to have ignored Dwight's injunctions, though he did pay one or two fines.

The Elers Brothers

Two brothers, David and Philip Elers, arrived as refugees from religious persecution in Holland at the same time as William of Orange. One had trained or worked as a jeweller and

▲ *David and John Philip Elers slip-cast red stoneware 'capuchine', decorated with a mould-applied flowering branch, c1695.*

the other was said to know the secrets of Cologne ware. They worked at the Fulham Pottery from 1690–3, then set up on their own in Bradwell Wood in Burslem, Staffordshire, perhaps under licence to John Dwight under the terms of his patent. He sued them on more than one occasion.

This pair really did have secrets which were destined to affect the tableware industry. The brothers made not salt glaze ware, but unglazed and polished red stoneware. Their range of tea and coffee items were much admired and sought after, firstly because of their excellent resistance to the heat of boiling water, but equally for their grace and delicacy, which fitted well with the refinements in domestic arrangements and arts which accelerated when Queen Ann came to the throne in 1702. Many of the Elers' pieces have applied silver rims or handles or knobs, which gives them an air of special value. Decorations also are sparingly applied and elegantly placed, so that there is never a suggestion of the rollicking tavernware that was more normal among the slip and lead glaze earthenware potters of not only Staffordshire, but all over the country.

There is nothing sloppy or unthinking about an Elers pot. Perhaps they were the first intellectually considered tableware. But as always, there was an external influence, and this one came, as had the inspiration for delft, many years earlier from China.

Yixing Teapots

Tea often arrived in chests that were also packed with small red teapots from the Yixing region of China, the tea giving a nice protection against the rigors of the long sea voyage. They are tough little pots anyway, with a long history in China, where they have always been highly valued for their perfect forms and perfect suitability for their purpose. Like the *mortaria* of the Romans or the posset pots of delft, they are utilitarian by design, by intention, by material. Anyone who has ever seen a Yixing 'Master' making one of these pots (they are hand-built, not thrown), can never forget the experience, and I doubt whether it matters whether the onlooker has an interest in clay or not. The Elers brothers had certainly seen these teapots, though whether this was before arriving in England or not seems unclear. They emulated rather than copied these wares, with a refined sensibility backed by consummate craftsmanship, and adapted the forms to the market environment in which they were working.

The brothers were as secretive as Dwight. They attempted to keep their productions from the general view of the potters of Burslem and the other nearby 'towns', but never stood a chance against a group of still largely uneducated, though skilled, artisans who considered

Yixing teapot. Chinese. Probably early twentieth century though the forms have been developed over thousands of years. The influence exerted by these small pots on potters in the West cannot be underestimated. On this fairly austere model, the little rings on the lid are not stuck down, but move quite freely and have an indented, rilled surface in contrast to the smooth body. The pot is not glazed at all, but there is no seepage because the fine orange-red clay has 'vitrified'.

it their birthright to know all if the subject was clay. The desire for secrecy and the taking out or attempted taking out of patents, can be seen firstly as indicative of a realization that wealth could be generated by a new, beautiful and better thing, and as an increase in the power of what had been very much an underdog profession through education and the dissemination of information.

Some rather farcical wrangling did ensue, though, as when someone attempted to take out a patent on Cornish stone, which is a naturally occurring clay, or when in 1736, fed up with wrangling potters and in front of a 'special jury of great wealth and intelligence' a judge finally said, 'Go home potters and make what you please'. This was in the face of a certain Ralph Shaw trying to take out a patent for chocolate-coloured salt glaze. Since salting was the only known glaze for stoneware there was a rush to develop different textures (the smoother the better) and colours.

Salt Glaze Declines

It might be thought that, since Astbury and Twyford, two of the clever Burslem potters, had discovered and were using the Elers methods in their own manufactories, that salt-glazed or unglazed stoneware might have been the products on which the industrial explosion of clay tableware in the following century would be based. That it was not the case was due in no small measure to another clever man with a scientific bent, Josiah Wedgwood. By the end of his lifetime salt glaze had gone the way of delft and visitors had no longer any need to fear the toxic fog the salt kilns of Stoke had produced on Saturdays for nearly a hundred years.

Left: a very early tin-glazed jug of the 'Malling' type, so called because some were found at Malling in Kent, c1630–40. Elizabeth I had allowed the settlement of large numbers of flax workers from the Low Countries during religious displacements over the latter part of the previous century. It may be that these jugs were bought from their home country to suit their taste, or they may have been made in Southwark in London, where there is known to have been an early tin-glaze workshop. Right: an English brown-glazed earthenware mug, c1650.

First, though, we must look back again to the beginning of the seventeenth century, when an elderly Elizabeth I reigned over her boisterous citizens, who suspected nothing of the need for heatproof cups as they breakfasted on cold beef and ale.

Earthenware

The Range of Shapes Broadens

Spurred on by the general economic and population growth, and with the added impetus of the example set by the 'fancy' delft tableware and of imports of better quality earthenware from the Continent, earthenware pottery workshops flowered from about the first quarter of the seventeenth century.

For the most part, this trade catered to the lower end of the market, but in places more remote from the great sea ports, a lively sense of place characterizes the ware, and the forms, more specific than ever before, include lots of dishes and platters that would not have been out of place on a country squire's table.

In the Midlands, the tradition of dark-glazed wares continued alongside yellow lead-glazed pots. Some of the black tankards, rilled horizontally in imitation of turned wood, are especially handsome and have been found as far apart as Abergavenny in Wales and Ely in East Anglia. They continued the restrained side of the earthenware tradition right up to the table revolution of the next century. Perhaps it was the unconscious memory of these pots that gave the luscious Japanese *tenmokus* such an easy entry into the English markets of the twentieth century. Many of the mugs were still multi-handled, so that members of the company could share their ale, but there were also many single-handled mugs and cups appearing, which, as the century wore on, became smaller, neater and lighter – thus more suitable for use in the dining room.

Wrotham Ware

A contrast to the quiet, sometimes elegant air of the Midlands slipped wares, were the Wrotham pots from Kent. These appear to be the first earthenware to be made where the decoration was more than incidental

Wrotham tyg for shared drinking, Thomas Ifield.

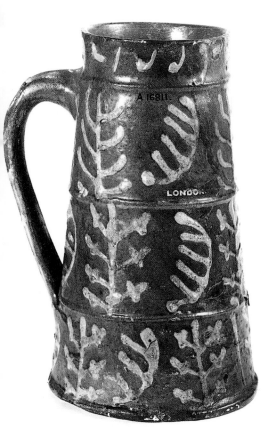

(except for painted delft). It has been suggested that this decoration was in imitation of the sprigs on the salt-glazed Cologne flagons, but if this was the case then the potters of Wrotham missed by miles, for the austerity that epitomizes the *bellarmines* is non-existent in the mugs, tankards, caudle pots, puzzle-jugs and candlesticks that were typical of their work. These pots are braided, sprigged, slipped, handled, initialled, dated, spotted, dotted, striped and have strange little buns of clay added as finials to the handles. They are also cheerfully and unpretentiously jolly. No one could possibly have shared a pint from one of them without experiencing a sense of well-being.

Metropolitan Ware

A new road, built between London and Newcastle early in the seventeenth century, made possible the growth of a group of potteries in the Harlow area of Essex. This ware is characterized by white slip trailing,

Metropolitan earthenware tankard from the Harlow area of Essex, found in London.

applied directly to the leather-hard clay without an intervening layer of slip, notoriously difficult to do on a tall, rounded shape. The patterns are decorous, even cautious, with evenly spaced zigzags, or herringbone or scrolled patterns. Many of the jugs, mugs and cups of this Metropolitan ware have been excavated in London, which would have provided the maker's largest marketplace.

In keeping with the Protestant sentiments that abounded around the time of Cromwell and in response to the terrors of both the Plague (1665) and the Great Fire of 1666, many of the mugs, jugs and chamberpots made by the Harlow potters have written exhortations to 'Fast and Pray' or 'God save us all'. Perhaps it was one of these less than cheerful mottoes that so irritated Mr Pepys when he was invited to dine at a banquet at the Guildhall, only to find that not only was he seated at rather a lowly place, but also that there were no napkins 'and we with wooden bowls and Earthen cups to drink from'. In common with most of the population, Mr Pepys loved a tipple. He was also a snob.

The potters of Harlow also made many earthenware dishes and plates elegant enough to be taken to the table in all but the best households. A flattish, wide shape is a pleasant one for a slipware potter to decorate, so a demand in the market could enlarge the potter's decorative potential.

The boiled puddings that had been around for a long time came, in the early seventeenth century, to be wrapped in a floured cloth, which meant that instead of being served with the meat in an intestine casing, they could be unrolled and served on a separate dish. A 'Hasty Pudding' recipe in Dorothy Hartley's wonderful book, *Food in England*, advises the pudding be 'put into a deep silver dish, or failing that one of brown earthenware'.

Sugar gradually became cheaper as plantations in British-owned colonies became established, so that puddings became sweeter and slowly replaced pottage as the rib-sticking cold-repelling food. By the middle of the next century pottage was food for the poor, and by the next, gruel for the workhouse.

North Devon Potteries

The potteries in Devon, at Bideford, Fremington and Barnstaple, cut their special local decorations through a layer of white slip, much as potters did in Beauvais in France. But there was nothing French about the results after generations of Devonian potters passed down this way of decorating to their children and their children's children. The large harvest jugs that became their hallmark were so special that they were kept in families as heirlooms, perhaps to be used only on festive occasions, but many more ordinary pots for kitchen and table were made as well. By the end of the seventeenth century, ships carried the products of these potteries to America, returning fully laden with tobacco.

Donyatt

Another very fine body of sgraffitoed earthenware pots came from Donyatt in Somerset. Here again, large numbers of plates and dishes, carefully made and decorated, testify to a gradually increasing role for earthenware as dining pieces rather than food preparation pots. The fact that the potters had the time and enterprise to make individual or special pieces further suggests a raising of customer expectation of quality and a better standard of living for the potter.

Earthenware Forms

Much of the coarseware made all over the country takes the same form because the pieces were to serve the same purpose, so are difficult to attribute to any particular pottery. The easiest to identify are those that represent not everyday pots for kitchen, dairy, farmyard or brewhouse but those that are of a commemorative nature; in such cases the potter exercised all his skill in the making and decorating of an individual piece that would give a sense of occasion when in use and where the meaning behind the image was known sometimes only to the community in which he worked, as with the slipped cradles made around Halifax, or the wassail bowls from the West Country.

Some other special pots bear images of the times in which potters lived and worked, records of momentous or shocking happenings in other parts of the country. None served this purpose better than the large thrown platters of the Tofts of Staffordshire.

In 1685, when Dr Plot visited this area from Oxford to record his *Natural History of Staffordshire*, he said that 'the greatest pottery they have in this country is carried on in Burslem near Newcastle-under-Lyme where for making several different sorts of pots they have many sorts of clay which is dug within half a mile of the town …' No doubt this gave the slip decorators here some edge. There was also a plentiful supply of wood, at least in the early part of the century, and later, when coal was used instead, there was plenty of that too. The lead for the glaze was mined in nearby Derbyshire. None of that would have sufficed without a little genius, born of consummate skill and a long tradition, and the Tofts had those to spare.

The themes of the platters and dishes are those shared with other decorative arts, religion, crests, emblems, coats of arms and with the painters of delft, but some stories were just better told in the flat areas of earthy colours, brown, buff, ochre and orange, edged with trails of a different tone and that pearled over with lines of tiny dots.

Particularly charming are those which depict Charles II's adventure in the Great Oak at Boscobel in 1651, where he hid for the whole day from the Roundheads. Thomas Toft

*M*odern earthenware slipped cradle with raised 'trailing' and little decorative buns of clay, Sue Neal, Kent. Raisins or other sweetmeats were served in these.

*H*oney pot, c1700. This probably came from Staffordshire.

has the royal head appearing, cheerful as a sparrow, through the branches. Charles never tired of telling this story, understandably, since he certainly would have been killed had he been caught and it is easy to imagine it appealing to the hearty, staunchly royalist potters of Burslem.

Catherine of Braganza, the same who bought her own tea things from Spain, is also portrayed in an endearing light, usually with her curly hair flying about and her crown perched at a jaunty angle. Ronald Cooper writes that these dishes must have adorned the homes of ardent royalists, perhaps on a cup-board or over a mantel, as did the delft chargers. They were not made as tableware, but the owner of one such dish told L. M. Solon, who was collecting them in 1850: 'This dish belonged to my Grandfather, and every year he served a Christmas pudding on it. Later it belonged to my father, and he too served a pudding on it each Christmas. It now belongs to me, and every year I has my Christmas pudding on it, and I don't want to part with it!'

It may be also that they were used as collecting plates for money given by guests at weddings. It would have been impossible to sidle by without noticing, and that is my excuse for including them in a book about tableware!

3 Towards Industry

I saw the field was spacious, and the soil so good, as to promise an ample recompense to any one who should labour diligently in its cultivation.

Josiah Wedgwood (1730–95)

During the sixteenth and into the seventeenth centuries, potters in Staffordshire were insulated by distance and the paucity of transport from the stoneware and Delft that found such large markets in the growing port areas of London, Bristol and Liverpool.

According to Peter Brears, historian and former Director of the Leeds City Museums, they 'used their own wit and initiative and practical experience of clay working instead

Braggart pot, Staffordshire. The lead-glazed earthenware is decorated in coloured slips. The simplest kind of braggart was made from ale, honey and powdered pepper only (C. Anne Wilson, Food and Drink in Britain*).*

WITHDRAWN

S *alt-glaze teapot, Staffordshire, c1720. The creamy body is off-set by the dip of lustrous iron-rich slip at the top. A salt-glazed stoneware jug with similar faceted sides on the lower half was found in a pre-1728 deposit at Williamsburg in the USA. The motifs have been applied from a metal die in the same way as on the red stoneware of the Elers brothers a few years previously.*

of attempting to imitate a better class of wares'. But they were forced to take on board new ideas throughout the eighteenth century in order to remain in an expanding but demanding marketplace.

In 1700 there were about forty pot houses in Burslem, mostly consisting of a potter and his family, some with apprentices and/or employees. They lived and worked in a collection of rough buildings next to their kilns, were heavily intermarried and knew what everyone else was doing. No wonder that the reticence of the Elers brothers was recorded in legend!

Several of the potteries, in addition to red, slipped earthenware, had begun to fire some grey, brown or cream salt-glaze ware, using the same kiln for both.

By the mid-nineteenth century, barely one hundred and fifty years later, not only Burslem but the surrounding villages had become an industrial complex whose task it was to put dishes, tureens, melon bowls, centrepieces, sauce boats, oyster pots and compotiers on the tables of eminent and not so eminent Victorians.

The wider causes of this revolution, so far-reaching in all areas of our lives, are beyond the scope of this study, since we are concerned with tableware from small workshops. However, contemporary hand makers utilize some of the innovations made during this important time, and there were a number of interesting characters involved. It must be pointed out also that standardization of raw materials, one of the basic tenets of production for the masses, was exceedingly difficult to achieve with pottery, so, by comparison with, say, the textile industry, very large factories were the exceptions rather than the rule. Potbanks varied greatly in the speed at which they mechanized, old and new existed side by side, and the hand of a maker is clearly in evidence on every early industrial pot pictured in this book.

The following are just a few of the factors that acted as stimuli to potters, as opposed to industry as a whole.

The Need for Daintier Tableware

In the first place, there was a dreadful hunger to find true whiteness and translucency as in the Chinese porcelains. John Evelyn, seventeenth-century diarist, wrote that 'invited by Lady Gerrard I went to London where we had a great supper; all the vessels which were innumerable were of porcelain, she having the most ample and richest collection in England.'

If the wealthy could not get whiteness and translucence in this country then they could afford to buy from China or the Continent where, under royal and court patronage, factories had been set up in Germany (Meissen) and France (Vincennes later Sèvre), but those among the middle classes who aspired to emulate Lady Gerrard were forced to be content with delft.

Many coaching inns, rumbustious and dangerous in the mid-eighteenth century when Henry Fielding wrote *Tom Jones*, became in the nineteenth-century establishments where ladies – properly chaperoned, naturally – could not only take a break from an arduous carriage journey, but also stay. It became fashionable to spend time in the new 'spas' and resorts, as did Jane Austen's heroines. People were travelling about the countryside more as well as taking trips abroad as in the 'Grand Tours' undertaken by those of means. Hotels in London and other cities began to cater for banquets and suppers where ladies might be present. The market for public tableware, durable, dainty and in quantity was ready and waiting.

Daintier, lighter wares were also demanded in the private houses of the urban merchants, middle classes and country gentry because the wider use of the stove and oven meant that the kitchen in Britain became the domain of women – women housekeepers, women cooks, women cleaners and women serving maids. The bearing into the dining hall of a whole spit-roast wild boar became a thing of the past, except at Oxbridge colleges.

French Influence Again

Although France was at war with England for much of the eighteenth and early nineteenth century, French ideas about food and manners continued to be in vogue, disseminated through the translations of books by chefs such as La Varenne, the most popular being called simply *The French Cook*. Food became lighter, the soup a thinnish vegetable broth based on the liquid in which meat or fish had been boiled.

At first, only the soup plates were 'removed' and diners helped themselves to the remaining dishes, which were served in two symmetrically arranged courses on the table, but by the early nineteenth century the fashion for serving 'à la Russe', where each dish with its accompaniments was bought separately to table, played right into the hands of the makers of tableware. Since dinners could be fourteen courses long, this serving method called for a great number of plates, dishes and bowls. There was no way that pottery could have serviced this demand as a home craft, any more than the spinning of yarn could satisfy the demand for cloth while based in crofters' cottages.

After the disruption to trade caused by the Napoleonic wars at the start of the nineteenth century, the domestic demand was augmented by that of the expanding New World. In the American states simplicity, clean, smooth surfaces and the durability to survive long journeys were all important. The Empire, too, provided an ever-expanding market. The potential was just waiting to be exploited.

Staffordshire Responds

In the potteries of Burslem and the other towns that now make up Stoke-on-Trent, the pace of change accelerated from about 1700 onwards. This is what L. M. Solon had to say about it, writing in 1883 '... the plodding, ingenious and practical potters of England, working as a body, succeeded in creating, by gradual transformations, a ware so superior to all others that the potting trade of all the world benefited by their exertions'. The ware he refers to is the earthenware called 'creamware', the culmination of a long line of improvements.

Thomas Astbury introduced ground flint stones into the clays of Staffordshire and a method was found of reducing the hazard of the dust by using water power – this was one of the first processes to be carried on away from the workshop. Ground flint was also found to be useful in combating the crazing often prevalent in glazes.

Ball clays and china clay – both vital for a white body – were brought by sea and packhorse from Devon and Cornwall, so earthenware and stoneware became paler, though the lead glaze on earthenware still retained a yellowish tinge.

The properties of Cornish stone, a decomposed granite rock and an important raw material, began to be investigated once it was established that no one owned the sole rights.

The Elers brothers had introduced lathe turning, a system of horizontally fixing the spinning pot so that it could easily be thinned and carved into, an adaption from wood turning. The brothers' particular contribution to improved pots was proving that with careful clay preparation to screen out all impurities, by lathe turning, and by careful firing, local clays could be made as smooth and as refined and light as anything brought from the mystic East.

Ralph Daniel of Cobridge, Staffordshire saw plaster of Paris in use at a factory in France. When it replaced the old carved pear wood moulds, a flood of inventive activity followed, especially with regard to teapots, which were becoming larger due to the decrease in the cost of tea. Some of the early press-moulded teapots display all the best characteristics of the coming together of the two materials, plaster and clay. Each section of, say, a square teapot body was pressed separately, slipped about the edges, then pressed onto the next piece. Watching a man using this method is, I am told, as gripping as watching someone throw well on the wheel. Aaron Wood was a particularly talented maker of the blocks for the early moulds. Although it is difficult to attribute pots themselves to him (since none were signed), some of the moulds are marked with his name – a measure of their worth. The industry benefited by his work since he provided moulds to almost all of the contemporary pot works.

The method of pouring liquid slip into a mould to 'cast' pots was utilized. A shape could be repeated exactly by a worker who required a specialist skill rather than overall craft training, at least for the making of the simpler shapes of tableware.

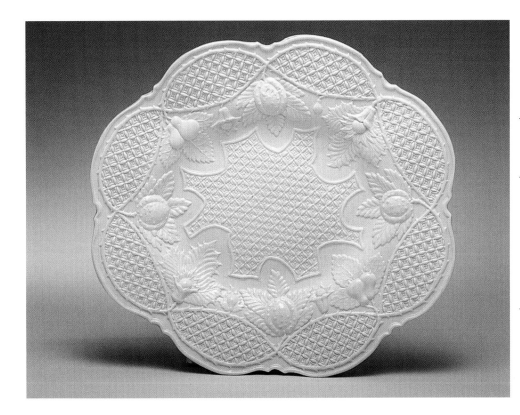

Salt-glaze plate, c1770. The plate has been press-moulded or cast. The moulds were taken from metal objects and the fabric is fine and hard. Three slight marks on the front show where the pot was propped on stilts face down in a saggar to protect its whiteness. It shows the great strides made in refining wares even before potworks were fully mechanized.

Improvements in Glazing Techniques

Enoch Wood improved the quality of lead glaze for earthenware and achieved an even, smooth application by dipping wares into a liquid suspension. A first or bisque firing facilitated this process.

Thomas Whieldon

Thomas Whieldon improved the earthenware clays in use. He stippled his pots with oxides of copper, iron or manganese before applying the glaze, and the resultant 'tortoiseshell' surface, in teaware, cups and plates, enjoyed such vogue that many copied the method. An order in Thomas Whieldon's book, from a Mr Thomas Fletcher, Dr, reads as follows:

1 doz. tortoiseshell plates,
2½ dozen plain plates (creamware)
2 teapots of the 'two dish' size, one painted, one plain
5 ice pails

By 1750 the use of the clay plate was commonplace, at least among the middle classes, though tea was still served in bowls or handleless cups.

Plate, Whieldon-type ware, c1770. The manganese decoration is 'splashed' under a clear lead glaze, and the plate is press-moulded.

Salt Glaze

Salt-glaze stoneware, initially rather drab buff and grey, became whiter, some decorated with 'scratch blue' cobalt decoration. These pots satisfied the demand for whiteness and could, after firing, be painted with enamels and fired to a lower temperature in a muffle kiln, so they were by no means all plain. Potters often shared the same 'enamellers', sending their moulded wares off by the crateload to be decorated. This salt-glaze ware also satisfied the need for a heatproof body. It was not by any means translucent, though, and the surface texture, even though the pots were put into special boxes or 'saggars' to be fired, always bore a slight roughness. The high firing temperatures and increasing cost of coal combined with the duty on salt that was imposed later in the century meant that salt-glaze ware could not be produced cheaply enough for the market. The standard of the ware deteriorated until, by about the same time as delft, it was edged out by a cream-coloured earthenware further improved by Josiah Wedgwood.

Loving cup, c1760. The cup is salt glazed with 'scratch blue' decoration in cobalt.

Josiah Wedgwood (1730–95)

Like Dwight in the previous century, Wedgwood was primarily a man of science. He was born into a potteries family of yeoman stock and received a basic education from his Unitarian mother, though he later relied heavily on the taste and refinement of his well educated partner and friend Thamas Bentley. The Ivy Works, his first pothouse, was still fairly much on the old model of house, with workshops and bottle kilns all in the same complex. It was here that creamware – a stronger, lighter earthenware – was perfected. Not only was this ware refined enough for even the most aspiring in society, but its cost was competitive, owing to Wedgwood's untiring attention to tools, techniques and labour. Through partnership with Thomas Bentley, Wedgwood gained access to the aristocratic clients he realized would benefit his business, and the two opened an upmarket showroom in London where new products were introduced and tableware in clay could be set out for viewing by prospective customers.

In 1769, Wedgwood was able to open a larger pot factory, based on his own ideas and improvements. This was on an estate between Hanley and Newcastle-under-Lyme and was called Etruria, after the Italian state whose ancient treasures were inspiring most of the decorative arts of the time.

Joseph Kenworthy (1852–1929) an enthusiastic local historian of the area, published a history of the Midhope potters of the West Riding of Yorkshire in 1928. Speaking of the demise of these potteries at the end of the eighteenth century he says 'Wedgwood [wares] by their beauty and neatness in the cupboard, to say nothing of cleanliness in everyday use, met a household want, and so swept aside such crude productions as Midhope earthenware off the table forever.'

*P*art of a Wedgewood dinner service. Earthenware, late eighteenth century. This creamware was renamed 'Queens's ware' by Wedgwood after prestigious sales of dinner services to royalty. The border and gold lines on this sample are handpainted on-glaze.

*J*asper teapot
c1790. Jasper
ware was
Wedgwood's most
truly innovative
contribution to
pottery and was
the culmination
of many years
of frustrating,
though ultimately
successful, trials
and testing. This
'Empire' style pot
was modelled by
William
Hackwood in
1785 though it
was designed,
along with many
other fashionable
pieces, by Lady
Templeton, one
of Wedgwood's
aristocratic
friends.

*C*aneware
'Solitaire' set,
Wedgwood.
Caneware was
perfected in about
1783 and was an
ideal medium for
producing items
which showed the
Oriental influence
prevalent at the
time. It was used
for a wide variety
of ornamental
wares. Even
this perfectly
functional teaset
for one may have
been intended as
a 'cabinet piece'.

In achieving this feat, that is, of satisfying the demands we looked at earlier, Wedgwood upgraded the status of British tableware in clay to unprecedented and dizzy heights: it was used by royalty, desired by the upper classes in Europe and the Colonies, bought in vast quantities for the finest establishments on the five continents. Even today, in a report for the Department of Trade and Industry by the Industries Research Group, it is stated that 'the name itself is a generator of business', meaning not only Wedgwood, which is now a large conglomerate, but other giants of the industrial revolution in ceramics such as Minton and Spode.

Other Whiteware

Spode

Josiah Spode it was who added ground bone to china clay to make that most English of translucent ware, bone china. This was used by polite society in the nineteenth century for the afternoon teas that gained in popularity as the hour for dinner, around noon in the sixteenth century, got later and later.

Porcelain

Porcelain of both the soft paste and hard paste varieties was manufactured at Chelsea, Bow, Derby, Worcester and Lowestoft among other places. The factory 'system' was introduced immediately, but even so the cost of these ornate and sometimes charming wares was always prohibitive. Only the Worcester factory lasted into the twentieth century. It was ironic that the quest for true porcelain had occupied the skills of so many, when, in much of the world, it was earthenware that became far and away the most widespread and economically important type of pottery.

Industry

As the rush for rationalization and the division of labour for increased profitability gathered pace, the old workshop ways were swept aside in this country as thoroughly as in other parts of continental Europe and America.

The quotation from Simeon Shaw below sums up the attitude of Georgian/Victorian England to the industrialization of Stoke-on-Trent, which by the time he wrote, in about 1830, was providing tableware and skilled labour to most of the Western world, but in common with other industries create an underclass of unskilled workers who were entirely divorced from the specialist tasks of designing or decorating.

> How pleasing to the Patriotic Philanthropist
> The landscape, with its devious hills and vales,
> Whose slopes exhibit many thousand roofs

The comfortable homes of laborants
Whose industry and art transmute to gold,
The copious stores of useful Minerals
Coals clays and ores derived from the mines
Enriching much their country and themselves.

This was written at a time when the Napoleonic wars had had a disastrous effect on the economy of the country and a series of very poor harvests worsened the lot of the urban poor, who, no longer able to brew the ale to which they were accustomed, took to drinking gin, which had become cheap after the lifting of import duties. Tea and coffee were still the preserve of the well-heeled.

The overstuffed interiors of Victorian England, combined with an obsessive dependence on designs from the past, and the desire to exhibit wealth with sheer volume caused a proliferation of design but not of quality in the nineteenth century. Clay had to be clothed expensively, leading to improved technical virtuosity at the expense of the basic material, clay.

After the American Civil War (1860–65), which caused a slump in exports from Stoke on Trent and from other places in Britain, potteries were set up in the American states, where design was rather better served by the general acceptance of undecorated ware, though for the top end of the market, blanks were imported from Stoke and decorated with transfer prints of more local interest.

Reaction

Every action has a reaction, so the scientists say, and there were voices of criticism of the design standards of ceramic products – including tableware – being made, particularly after some of the big trade fairs which were influential in the nineteenth century.

In reply, both Doulton and Minton set up 'Art' workshops. The former was especially successful though financed largely by other parts of the company. The grip of manufacturing on tableware was tight, and in retrospect suffocating; even the famous Martin Brothers did not seriously attempt to compete.

It was the Arts and Crafts movement that complained most bitterly about the disastrous effects of the machine age on all the decorative arts, but their ideals were rooted in an over-romantic view of a glorious medieval revival of the long-since replaced workshops, where men could enjoy the simplicity and nobility of the lifestyle that would accompany the making of hand-crafted goods – furniture, textiles, pots, metalworking and so on. The leading exponents of the theories which inspired these high ideals were John Ruskin (1819–1900) and William Morris (1834–96).

Since the protagonists of this movement, certainly where ceramics were concerned, were largely enlightened gentlemen and ladies who felt no more need than the industrial entrepreneurs to get their hands dirty by actually making pots themselves, their main contribution was that of elaboration, in glaze and decoration. The work of making the pots themselves was usually carried out by a labourer. Wares were to be viewed rather than used, were 'Art', rather than craft. The design and decoration were all important.

Some art potters, such as Adelaide Robineau in America or the eccentric Sir Edward Elton in England, did make for themselves, but it was by no means standard practice. At the Lindthorpe pottery in Middlesborough, where the designer realized that the pots would have more life by being hand-worked, pots from the wheel were pushed into wooden moulds in order to perfect the shape for the decorators. Much interesting work was done on glaze and colour and the output of the art potteries varied from crude to stunning. Useful it mostly was not.

The Workshops

Many coarseware eathenware potters, with skills learnt in Stoke on Trent but no longer required there, set up workshops unnoticed by all but the urban and rural poor who continued to patronize them. Skilled workers also took themselves to America, Australia and further afield, where they were joined by fellow potters from other parts of Europe.

At the end of the nineteenth century there were about eighty small establishments run on the old lines, up and down the country, supplying pots to poor communities. Sometimes these pots were particular to an area.

In the West Country potteries continued to make fat 'bussas' for brining pilchards, on which the fishermen of Devon and Cornwall depended as a staple food during the winter.

A wonderful story is told of the potters of north Devon racing down to the quayside, their carts laden with these big pots, when news arrived of the arrival of the fishing fleet. Apparently the Lakes Pottery of Truro invariably arrived first because the horses of the other potters stopped, as was their habit, outside every pub on their way to the shore.

In America, especially in remote areas where country potteries had established early and were integrated into rural life, country potters also continued to eke out a living in spite of industry. Jugs for moonshine and whisky and jars for preserving and pickling continued to be made, but there was no point in making tableware this way.

*P*ancheon, probably Buckley, North Wales, late nineteenth/early twentieth century. These pots were made in many sizes by coarseware potters all over the country for kitchen and dairy. Dorothy Hartley in Food in England *gives a recipe for a rook pie to be cooked in a dish of this sort. It begins 'A rook pie is not worth making unless some large rookery has to be thinned, when it is a pity to waste the bag of young birds bought in by the countrymen.'*

Dish, possibly from Sunderland, early twentieth century. The dish is press-moulded with a slabbed divider. The body is dark, with a clear glaze and white slip decoration. The back is heavily marked by fire.

New Materials

In urban areas everywhere, the crocks that had been used for centuries were eventually replaced by new packaging of cheaply produced glass and tinplate.

Canned foods were first invented to feed troops overseas but householders soon caught on to the labour-saving advantages. The cook in 1900 might still be able to prepare a sheep's head for broth and a main course, but she could get bottled anchovy or tomato sauce, packets of custard powder, or cans of meat from the overseas colonies. In terms of health and protection from famine, these products were invaluable. Long winters would never be the same, but the implications for the potteries were, along with a cheaper and faster transport system, disastrous.

Potters did try innovations in order to stay in the markets of the time with varying degrees of success. Some went into rather sad gift wares, some into the fashionable 'Art' wares, some into ceramics for construction and drainage. The Fulham Pottery, founded so long ago by John Dwight, made drink bottles for the Boer War and bed-warmers for the Crimean.

It was at one of the surviving pot works in north Devon that the young Michael Cardew, at the beginning of this century, watched Edwin Beer Fishley throwing and slip decorating his pots. The boy was said to have become very cross when it was time to go home, even kicking his nurse on one occasion. Although he went on to study at Oxford he never lost his early enthusiasm and was to become one of the pioneers of the modern Studio Pottery movement.

Perhaps the old potteries might still be in production and now fashionable were it not for the two World Wars. Those sons of potters who once may have carried on with the trade of their fathers, when they did come back were not prepared for the hardships attendant on the lifestyle and went on to less arduous occupations. And who can blame them?

4 The Twentieth Century

*Our sensibility to beauty is ministered for the most part
only by the work of a handful of men of genius …*

Bernard Leach, *A Potter's Book*

The First Decades

At the beginning of the twentieth century, the Arts and Crafts movement's ideal of traditional works being produced by craftsmen in small, preferably rural, workshops for the edification of the masses continued to confuse. The emphasis remained on artist-designers. Already in both America and France there was a growing band of independent potters, who carried out all ceramic processes themselves without employing labour to do the dirty bits or a painter to embellish or a chemist to devise the glaze.

There were plenty of potteries in Britain, as elsewhere, inspired by new glaze effects, decorations and styles such as art nouveau. These potteries used industrial or mass production methods to cater to society's demand for 'Art' wares, which usually meant wares produced by industrial or mass production methods but designed by an artist.

Many of the forms were either rooted in the past (mediaeval and Gothic were popular) or were designed for novelty – the clay forced into the most extraordinary shapes and heavily disguised by an ornate covering. The public seemed to have an insatiable taste for unusual glazes – lustres, crackles in gold or silver, reduced copper reds, streaked effects in flamboyant reds and greens, bright blues and browns overlaid to run perfectly into each other, crystalline glazes of kingfisher blue or uranium orange, flambés and soufflés and some bearing 'a curious resemblance to mould growths'. Some potteries made 'grotesque' lines of strange animals in the form of teapots or jugs or tankards, while yet others were intricately carved and painted. There are many, of course, that exhibit great artistic merit, particularly from American potteries, where unity of form, surface and ornament (or lack of it) prevailed, but there are very few pieces from which you would want to eat even a biscuit and cheese. That was not why they were made. The people who desired and bought these pots all went home to eat from a dinner service from a well-known manufacturer, more than likely one based in Stoke-on-Trent. Because people now tended to live in

*P*ress-moulded
platter with
meringues, Janice
Tchalenko, 1980s.
Coloured glazes have
been applied to
reduced stoneware.

smaller houses or flats in urban areas, the standard service had been reduced from one hundred to fifty pieces. For those wanting to set up in a small workshop, there was simply no point in making tableware because there was no demand.

There was at the same time a demand for better education in the decorative arts in general. In America, the Alfred School was set up in New York State in 1900 to cater especially for ceramics. All aspects – technology, design and decoration – were to be taught under one roof to the benefit of both industry and craft. The era of the artist-designer who never touched a clay bin was coming to an end. The old way, of training by apprenticeship and work experience, has never died, nor will it, but the access to wider information that informs the work of potters today has transformed a craft into an art, for tableware no less than any other field. There were several art schools in the UK where the subject was taught but they were either fine art or design-oriented, or concentrated on technology, like those based in Stoke on Trent. Pottery as serious study occupied a very lowly place in the art hierarchy.

What was needed to elevate its position was a philosophical foundation, a sense of importance and of worthwhile endeavour. This ultimately came from the East as had so many stimuli to potters in the past, in the person of Bernard Leach.

The New Generation

ROGER FRY AND THE OMEGA WORKSHOPS

Already a decade before Leach's return, Roger Fry, an energetic and well-travelled art critic and former curator of painting at the Metropolitan Museum in New York, had also been lured to clay, and though his convictions lay in other directions, his admiration for the clean lines and pure surfaces of Sung ware from China and his writings helped to cast a new light on ceramics, if only in the elevated artistic circles in which he moved.

'That the art of pottery in England, which began with such noble and serious work should have degenerated into cheerful brutality on the one hand and empty elegance on the other is surely deplorable ...', Roger Fry commented, reviewing an exhibition of English stoneware and earthenware organized by the Burlington Fine Art club in 1914.

His answer was to set up the Omega Workshops in 1913, influenced in this by similar ventures he had witnessed for himself in France. The idea was that if real artists designed and painted, or decorated everyday things – cushions, carpets, fabrics, tableware – then this would encourage the public to take an interest in and to be alive to art itself. Like William Morris in the century before, he and his friends believed there had to be an antidote to the stultifying, overblown bad taste that was exemplified in many cases by the group's Victorian childhood homes and upbringings.

Fry had set up the first exhibition of French Impressionist paintings in London in 1910 and the utter disdain of the critics had served to isolate him somewhat from the mainstream of serious art and talking about it. Once he decided that pots would have a place in the Omega range, he took himself off to a thrower in Surrey, then to Poole Pottery in Dorset, and then to Camberwell School of Art in London to learn to throw on the wheel.

In this he fared moderately well, considering the brevity of his apprenticeship, but the zest and joyful sense of purpose with which the Omega artists decorated these rather unrefined and clumpy pots must have been a revelation to those accustomed to the over-dressed products of the art wares that had been the vogue. The clay was even allowed to show

through the glaze, which was usually either tin to allow the maximum colour response or left plain to show off the forms, as in the Chinese Sung wares.

Quentin Bell, the son of one of the leading decorators, Vanessa Bell, who himself later became a potter, said that the pots had 'a gentle warmth' and it is a warmth that speaks of life's pleasures. The vases are for bunches of spring flowers and the jugs are for milk, the plates for eating from, or, if the glaze is not fired quite well enough, for brightening up a patch of wall. There is a particular Englishness about the cohesion of pattern and palette in an Omega interior and the pots are only a small part of that, not works of art in themselves but because of their association with that most fundamental human activity, eating, they are integral parts of that work of art (if we are fortunate) that is living.

*O*mega sauce *boat, Roger Fry, c1915. The earthenware is covered in a milky tin glaze. The piece is marked on the base.*

VANESSA AND QUENTIN BELL

Later, after Omega had disappeared, another victim of the 1914 war, Vanessa Bell and Duncan Grant had pots made or cast for them by a potter, Phyllis Keyes. Quentin then took over, became a potter and continued the family tradition of making pots to please himself and those around him – homely likeable pots that often uphold his view that there is 'a quite considerable place for vulgarity in life'. The Charleston style set by this group gained some following. Quentin had potters and students work with him and it is good to see echoes of pattern and colour in the work of some younger makers of tableware.

KATHERINE PLEYDELL BOUVERIE

Katherine Pleydell Bouverie, who later worked with Bernard Leach and went on to experiment with ash-based glazes, making some very beautiful vases and bottles and bowls in the process, became interested in clay while watching Roger Fry throwing at Camberwell. The widespread use of the Omega motif for book covers, fabrics and furniture make it not unreasonable that there are sometimes traces of the style to be seen in the decorated stoneware of Michael Cardew later on.

WILLIAM STAITE MURRAY

William Staite Murray taught at the Royal College of Art in the 1920s. He produced some monumental pots, all vessel based, though having nothing to do with tableware. He was instrumental in raising the profile of the craft of pottery, a pioneer artist potter who charged high prices for his work because he considered himself a true artist. All this helped, not only to focus some attention on clay, but to encourage a small but enthusiastic band of collectors and admirers.

BERNARD LEACH

Most of today's tableware potters, from all parts of the English-speaking world, will readily acknowledge a debt to Bernard Leach for the existence of the craft they practise. Through his writings and teachings he made the work of the Studio Potter not only valid, but (provided certain standards were maintained) morally and spiritually the 'right path'. As with many admired leaders, timing and circumstance played their part, as well as the artist's indomitable spirit and a sense of evangelizing fervour.

Leach spent some time immersed in ceramics in the Far East, where he entered into partnership with Japanese Shoji Hamada. Hamada, the technician in the partnership, accompanied Leach on his return to England in 1920. After many trials and tribulations they set up the workshop in St Ives in Cornwall to make, on the one hand, slip-decorated, galena-glazed earthenware in the manner of early English potters, whose way of life and work fitted their idea of moral and artistic right. On the other hand, they made high-fired stoneware very much in the Eastern tradition, inspired by Chinese Song and Korean Yi dynasty wares.

There is a sad little piece in *The Potter's Book* about the early earthenware, although collectors admired it here and it was appreciated greatly in Japan, where Leach continued to exhibit:

> … after the fever of technical research had abated, we saw that there were definite limitations to the use of slipware in present-day life. The softness and relative roughness of the ware relegates it for the most part to the kitchen and the cottage in the shape of casseroles, bowls, egg-bakers, honey pots, oven dishes, jugs, pitchers, basins and so forth, although its great decorative value opens for it the way to many other uses. But few people want red and brown or black or heavy creamcoloured ware for table use in modern cities.

All of the pots were very much in the artist-craftsman mould, one-off pieces only functional by accident, though all based on vessel forms or platters. There were many problems during this time, technical as well as financial, but some very beautiful pieces came from the kiln, such as the magnificent Leaping Salmon vase now in the York City Art Gallery.

TABLEWARE AT ST IVES

After the depression of 1930s money was very tight. In order to make some attempt at breaking even, the pottery was encouraged to consider making a range of table or useful wares.

It so happened that in 1928 a friend of Leach, the Japanese philosopher and critic Yanagi, had come to visit St Ives and given moral purpose to a necessity because he praised above all usefulness in craft works, for there lay the foundation of all real art and beauty. In fact Yanagi was familiar with the works of Ruskin and William Morris and based his 'Mingei' philosophy, which praised the unknown craftsman, on their teachings. (From unpublished papers given by Yuko Kikuchi and Edmund de Waal, 1998)

David Leach, Bernard's son, then went to Stoke-on-Trent for the technical training that Bernard himself lacked, and this helped ensure the success of the range of simple, useful forms that were produced at the pottery for many years.

Michael Cardew arrived to work at St Ives in 1923 and he went on to found the pottery at Winchcombe, which was taken over in turn by Ray Finch and his son. Cardew also built up a pottery at Wenford Bridge in Cornwall. These two potteries, with St Ives, then trained and sent back to all corners of the world a great many dedicated potters of functional pots and tableware. Even if they then took on influences from other sources and made pots that look unrelated, they shared the underlying philosophy – that the making and using

Oval stoneware bowl, Shoji Hamada, c1960. Note the tenmoku glaze over clear, with six resist roundels. Leach was a great communicator, but Hamada was a gifted and inspirational maker, and was as much a founder of the modern studio pottery movement as his friend and partner.

*C*offee pot, c1960. The impressed St Ives seal proclaims the origins of this tenmoku-*glazed* pot (left).

*J*ug, c1950. The pale oatmeal coloured stoneware is again identified by the St Ives seal.

*C*offee pot, c1960. The impressed St Ives seal proclaims the origins of this tenmoku-*glazed* pot (left).

*J*ug, c1950. The pale oatmeal coloured stoneware is again identified by the St Ives seal.

of pots that show the hand of the maker and the nature of the materials can be full of promise of all that is humane and generous in life. Integrity and truth are all important.

The list of these 'apprentices' is far too long to plough through but the reader can be assured that whether the hand-made tableware in the cupboard has been collected in New Zealand, Australia, America, Canada, South Africa or any other of the countries visited by Leach, the chances are that more than half of it has been made by a potter taught at first, second, or by now even third hand, by one of these pioneer studio potters. Even more would testify to being influenced or inspired, or both, by *A Potter's Book*, first published in 1940.

The Post-War Years

It was a piece of good fortune that the St Ives pottery was allowed to continue during the 1939–45 war while many others were forced to close for one reason or another. After the war, the pottery was in an enviable situation vis-à-vis the provision of interesting and different tableware to a population heartily sick of the plain white utility wares imposed on them by the necessities of wartime. Heals, John Lewis, Liberty, Peter Jones and other large stores took as much stock as they could get and as the economic situation slowly improved, so galleries opened and exhibitions became more frequent.

The Aftermath of War

The two World Wars made changes to lifestyles quite out of proportion to their duration. The formalities of Edwardian society gave way to a much more casual and comfortable style. The fine bone china matching tableware that could be left for the servants to wash gave way to practical everyday crockery for use in more modest establishments. And potters of hand-crafted pots were able to take advantage.

What had been limited to Oriental-inspired, rather rustic and romantic selections from a few potters in the 1930s became a growth area of great potential. New design ideas from the Continent – filtered from Modernist movements – brought more natural and neutral interiors. The colours and textures of stoneware fitted the bill perfectly, as did brown *tenmokus*, stony oatmeal or matt white dolomite glazes, often with unglazed sections to show the basic material as other craft workers were doing in their disciplines.

The demand for useful pots was great and it was no accident that while the boom lasted the throwing skills of many production potters working today became prodigious. A course designed specifically for training production potters was set up in the late 1960s at Harrow by Michael Casson and Victor Margrie. This satisfied a need for an alternative to the apprenticeship system and was an added educational benefit to those who felt the need for further intensive training, perhaps after a stint at a working pottery. These were people whose minds were set on making pots for the table or kitchen as a career. Its graduates are among the finest ceramic artists of this era and have proved to be inspirational to others who practice the craft.

Other Influences

As we have seen, educational possibilities widened during Leach's lifetime, so that while the potters receptive to his teachings at the time exhibited enthusiasm and courage, the second generation was a well-grounded and motivated cross-class generation of would-be functional potters willing to learn but also keen to question.

In part, the questions were informed, as so often in the past, by ideas that had come from Continental Europe in the wake of the upheavals of the first half of the century.

LUCIE RIE

Lucie Rie came to settle in Britain in 1937 seeking refuge from growing Nazi power in her home country, Austria. Her interests and background could hardly have been more different from those of Bernard Leach in that she was an urban sophisticate, a child, though she never studied there, of Bauhaus modernism, which encompassed concepts of simple, austere and minimal design and a commitment to allowing materials and methods speak for themselves.

She was already a working potter with a growing reputation in Vienna so it must have been difficult to work effectively in a country where she was forced literally to begin again, with the ideas current on the pottery scene here tied to the traditional and rural. Throughout a long working life in London, Rie made pots based on functional forms – bowls, vases and bottles, pots meant for domestic interiors. But it was in the 1950s and 60s when Studio Pottery was so popular that she and Hans Coper, who was at the time working with her, made the most of the fashion and produced some of the finest studio tableware produced in this century; the forms are strong yet flowing, distinctively thrown and turned and covered in either white mattish or tin glazes, or, on exteriors rhythmic 'cages' of sgraffito cut through chocolatey manganese pigments. They are pots at peace

*B*owl, Lucie Rie, c1960. The impressed seals are LR and HC on this stoneware piece with its speckled white/oatmeal glaze.

*C*offee set and bowls, Lucie Rie, c1970. The glaze contains tin, with manganese banding to the rims.

with themselves, without fuss, though meticulous attention to detail was visibly important. Rie herself was 'without fuss' and as strong in character as her pots were in form.

She taught, apparently unwillingly, wrote nothing, was 'indifferent to theory' (her own words) and was 'just a potter', unlike Hans, who was an artist potter. Margaret Cuddon, in a tribute written in *Ceramic Review* on the death of Lucie Rie in 1995, wrote:

> I love the form of her pots, her beautiful shapes, the miraculous thinness, the textures and colours. Her work makes me think of a perfect dinner prepared by a super-cook. The ingredients have been carefully and lovingly chosen and prepared and the architecture of the meal is right on – a balance of taste, textures and colours, put together with consummate skill and presented with concern for detail. The result is not, happily, eaten within the hour. With great good fortune and tender conservation it will be a joy forever.

Rie's pots were never intended to be put away, in spite of their modesty. They are all useful in household terms and an air of ordered calm seems to settle around them. An acquaintance told me a few years ago that he had a brown coffee set by some potter on top of the cupboard in a box. Would I come and see if it was worth anything? He had bought it in the late 1950s when he was studying architecture in London. Of course that was a clue, but I did not register it. When a fine Rie coffee set appeared from the box, I twisted his arm to make coffee immediately, set out the pieces and found digestive biscuits for the plate, milk for the side-handled jug and sugar for the bowl. It was an experience as elegant as tea at the Ritz.

Making Pots Today

Michael Cardew was told that in Japan it takes seven years for a potter to learn to throw and twenty to set up a viable pottery. He concluded after many years' work that that was about right. It is no accident that none of the potters represented in this book is under thirty years of age. Given the now huge and burgeoning accumulated body of writing, videos, internet clay sites and circuit lectures and workshops, it is still possible, with dedication, to go it alone without the benefit of formal education in school or with an established potter, but this certainly would mean years of either independent financial support or else real economic deprivation. Today's market, whether in the USA, Canada, Australia or New Zealand, is difficult, with customers more discerning than ever, much more so than in the brown pot time of the 1960s. Earning a living can be hazardous without another prop – teaching is popular for that reason. But whether the potter works full time in a rowdy university setting, in a busy workshop, alone in an urban studio, or perhaps in a two-person partnership in an isolated country pottery, he would no doubt cite the lifestyle associated with the profession as one reason for persisting. It certainly is not the money.

The idea of educating the masses to the nature of art, or the return of the country artisan as the high ideal of society, as propounded by the Arts and Crafts movement or indeed by Bernard Leach, has largely been superseded by more practical attitudes. Potters today do not see themselves as competing with industry, but as offering an alternative, and if that means catering to a small, well-educated and artistically aware elite then so be it.

Gwari stoneware casserole, Michael Cardew, c1970. The impressed seals are MC and Wenford Bridge. Incised through a mottled green and brown glaze. Katherine Pleydell-Bouverie said of Michael Cardew in Ceramic Review: *'He has written one of the best books on the making of pots in the English language. And he has made pots. His odd and erratic career is littered with them. Steeped in tradition, but tradition always freely used; pots made because the potter wanted to make them; made for use; idiosyncratic, sometimes funny, often splendid.'*

Anyway, it is recognized that not all industrial wares are 'thin, mean and hard' as described by Leach. There is a place for the machine-made and a place for the hand-made. There have been in the past and will always be fruitful comings together of design and machine, which illustrate that all is not lost just because the market is huge and must be serviced.

But it must be said that the uniformity is depressing, and the mug rack in the local supermarket a weekly reminder that things could be better. After seeing it, usually by accident, I have to go home and read again Roger Fry's observation (in the undated catalogue to the Omega Workshops, now in the Victoria and Albert Museum) that 'the artist [read tableware potter] is the man who creates not only for need but for joy, and in the long run mankind will not be content without sharing that joy through the possession of real works of art, however humble or unpretentious they may be.'

In the preceding chapters I have attempted to show the historical background of today's tableware potter. It is no longer possible or even desirable to make a totally unselfconscious pot, one that is utilitarian without the benefit of 'art' as potters did long ago, but it is also impossible for us unselfconsciously to place a less honoured guest at the bottom of the table to eat the entrails of the deer while we eat the haunch (eating humble pie), or to kiss the hem of somebody's cloak. A favourite motto for institutions of learning is 'knowledge is power', and it is impossible to believe that the accumulated knowledge of the workings of clay, which after all these centuries still holds mystery, cannot, with dedication and a sense of curiosity and invention, produce yet more magical objects that beg to be filled with food, emptied and admired.

II

CONTEMPORARY POTS FOR TABLES

From being a useful tool to assist in the better survival of mankind, ceramic or clay tableware came, in some parts of the world, to be symbolic of power, wealth and discernment.

When Catherine the Great of Russia ordered the famous 'Frog Service' in creamware from Josiah Wedgwood in the 1770s she was establishing her financial and social superiority over both her own court and people and visiting foreign dignitaries. This dinner service for fifty people consisted of 952 pieces, an incredible average of nineteen pieces for each diner. Each piece was hand-painted with a different English scene, as well as the frog logo and a simple border pattern.

This is the attitude that has prevailed in most parts of the West, with a selection of best china still put away in a cabinet or dresser for use on occasions of importance, even in many ordinary households.

At the other end of the spectrum we have taken on board the idea that the receptacle that holds our food is of no importance whatsoever and is better discarded after the meal. A banana leaf suffices in parts of India. In the same country some Hindi castes ritually smash the pots used after a meal – which does not give a great deal of incentive to potters and is completely at odds with the durability that we take for granted as desirable in clay pots.

The materials for our throwaways will no doubt improve and take over further areas, especially of public food consumption, but it is to be hoped that old habits will die hard and that to own something beautiful, more interesting or special to hold our food will continue to have a place in our lives, on a daily basis as well as for meals that celebrate rites of passage.

This section examines the forms we presently use for dinnerware. Some of them have been used since time immemorial, some are relatively new. Fashion and food together dictate the shapes, but potters from studios and workshops are in a unique position to interpret them in ways that increase our intimate relationship with the food we eat and thus add to the enjoyment.

*S*mall bowls, Jane Cox, London, 1998. Made on a jolley fixed to a wheel head. The vibrancy of colour is possible because the underlying clay is white. Fired in an electric kiln.

5 Bowls

*No basic pottery shape emphazises harmonic principles more clearly than
the open bowl, a popular shape historically, functionally, aesthetically.*

Tony Birks, *The New Potter's Companion*

According to Greek legend, the first bowl was moulded over the breast of Aphrodite. The connection is an apt one for of all the forms made for the table the bowl is the most symbolic of comfort and succour – of hot soup on a cold winter's night or of a cooling fruit salad in the heat of the afternoon in summer. The word in English is very old, dating at least from Saxon times, and its use as a description of a shared drinking vessel (as in the popular song below) also gives it an air of conviviality, which has been continued with wassail bowl and punchbowl:

Salad in a bowl, Janice Tchalenko, early 1980s.

Come landlord fill the flowing bowl
Until it doth run over.
For tonight we'll merry, merry be.
Tomorrow we'll be sober.

Tin-glazed earthenware, Linda Arbuckle, Florida.

The Chinese have many different words for bowls in order to describe differences in shape or use, and so do we. A dish is flatter, a basin taller and used for more mundane purposes, for washing or mixing batters or bread dough. 'Bowl' is often qualified to give a clearer picture – for example, finger bowl, mixing bowl, soup bowl. Now that there are fewer rules (though they still exist as habits, rather than rules) covering the uses of items of tableware, bowls are utilitarian in the widest sense. They are capable of holding foodstuffs from the very liquid to the very dry, and so users of potters' bowls choose individual pieces for whatever purpose suits their particular requirements.

Vegetarian food often favours a bowl or dish over a plate; it is much easier to catch your bean sprouts in something with a decent rising edge. In countries where rice is the staple food, bowls have long been preferred. With the spread of these different types of foodstuffs it would make sense for potters to seize the opportunity and make larger individual bowls. Those pictured here by Daphne Carnegy and Hilary Roberts are in constant use, especially for meals involving pasta or rice.

Tin-glazed earthenware, Oliver Dawson, East Sussex.

White on white glazed porcelain, Hilary Roberts, West Yorkshire.

*T*in-glazed
earthenware,
Daphne Carnegy,
London (left).

*W*hite
slip-covered
earthenware with a
clear glaze, Judith
Rowe, London.

Before the importation of Ming bowls from China in the sixteenth century, those made by local potters tended to be rather crude and only for the tables of the poorest, for kitchen and dairy or for implements related to hand washing. Even the tin-glazing delft potters did not appear to favour the shape, perhaps preferring the decorative possibilities of the new-fangled flatware, though their punch bowls, footed in the Chinese manner, are often masterpieces of the craft.

*R*eduction fired
stoneware, Karen
Ann Wood, Kent.

Making Bowls

Bowls can be made from clay in even more ways than plates. They can be moulded in a plaster shape, jolleyed – where a simple shape is compressed into a plaster former on the wheel head – slip-cast, or even just pinched from a small ball of clay in much the same way as our distant ancestors must have done when the necessity arose. Bowls can also be coiled using rolled sausages of clay, applying them on top of each other then smoothing and scraping till the form is felt to be right. Both the last two options are very labour intensive, too much so for a workshop dependent on efficient production.

Throwing

Bowls are truly sensational to make on a turning wheel, and it is no accident that a learner's first pleasing pot is invariably a bowl. The spinning of the wheel throws an attached mound of plastic clay outward almost by itself and the maker looks into a recognizable hemispherical shape before he can believe it has happened. A skilled thrower can make small bowls at an incredible pace. Demonstrations of wheel throwing in public places usually involve bowl-making for that reason, and because of the wide tolerance of form in what we consider a bowl to be. The variations for the viewer are many, but they are endless for the thrower.

To make useful, containing bowls is not difficult. To make beautiful bowls is another matter entirely and one that exercises the mind of a thoughtful maker long after he has mastered the art of drawing the clay into a semicircular shape.

Bowls can exhibit a variety of moods according to their form. A rim turned inward even slightly will make a bowl rather secretive – more likely to be used as an occasional holder for liquids, sauces or dressings. A bowl with the rim turned out is inviting and hospitable.

S lip-painted earthenware, Sophie MacCarthy, London (Opposite, above).

S mall bowls, tin-glazed earthenware, Posey Bacopoulos, New York (Opposite, below).

S mall bowls, reduced stoneware, Karen Ann Wood, Kent.

W ood-fired reduced stoneware, Winchcombe Pottery, Gloucestershire.

F ooted bowl, with thick white slip-trailed decoration, Takeshi Yasuda, North Devon, 1980s.

REQUIREMENTS

If bowls are intended for hard use on kitchen tables as well as in the dining room, perhaps for cereals or soups, then even more regard should be given to their function. For example, a turned or applied footring under a bowl gives a sense of lift and lightness. If it is either too high or too narrow for the maximum width of the form it will make the bowl into purely a party piece

S mall bowl, wood-fired reduced stoneware, Svend Bayer, Devon.

B ase of the bowl above showing comfortable footring, round-edged to complement the bowl. The pale marks are left by wads of refractory material which separate the clay from the kiln shelf during the firing.

because stability will be affected. The bowl will lurch unexpectedly if food is dug into without the use of a steadying hand. A footring should complement the shape of the bowl. Too heavy, thick or square a footring is rarely satisfactory.

Rims are best not too thin as their width compared to the body of the pot makes them vulnerable to chipping. I have a friend who owns a wonderful old French country bowl that is chipped all round. She continues to use it, but I suspect her loyalty is not shared by many. As with

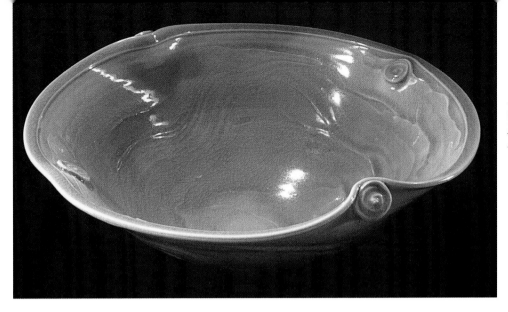

Porcelain bowl, thrown and altered, Joanna Howells, Mid-Glamorgan.

plates, throwing rings (those marks left by the fingers inside pots when they are made on the wheel) are best removed from the interior surface if the pot is intended for a wide range of uses, and the glaze on the inside should be smooth and well fired.

The width of the rim of a bowl means that in the making, support usually comes from a broad, thick base. If it is not excessive, this extra thickness can be removed with a pointed tool while the pot is still on the wheel head. The bowl is then cut from the wheel head using a piece of wire or string and the pattern so made remains as evidence after the pot has been fired and completed.

TRIMMING OR TURNING A BOWL

Often the thrower has only completed the inside shape, the rim and some of the outside at this stage. When the bowl has firmed to leather hard it is replaced on the wheel head upside down and 'turned' to shape the exterior. The interior is no longer visible and so

Handled bowl, soda-fired, Ruthanne Tudball, Berkshire.

*S*alad bowls, once-fired earthenware, Josie Walter, Derbyshire.

memory and judgement come into play. If the memory of what is hidden is wrong then an unbalanced bowl is the sure result.

Porcelain clays in particular often require a long time in the turning. It is the incredible fired strength of porcelain that allows it, when required, to be turned to a thinness that would be impossible and undesirable in other stoneware or in earthenware.

Bowls in Use

The picking up and putting down of a bowl should be easy and natural, one-handed in the case of a cereal bowl. Excessive weight or unwieldy shapes will again condemn the bowl to the cupboard or shelf. There are some bowls, though, for example Linda Arbuckle's vibrant yellow beauty pictured on page 77, that would be impossible to put away. It demands to be noticed. And after all, one of the many functions of bowls in our society is visual. The fact that the possibility of participation in food serving and sharing exists serves to heighten the aesthetic impact.

6 Jugs and Pitchers

There is perhaps only one occasion on which English potters have developed a new idea of importance – that is the idea of the mediaeval jug.

K. J. Barton, *Pottery in England from 3500 BC–AD 1750*

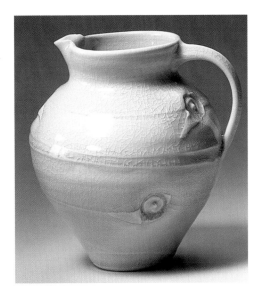

It is easy to see why the above statement was made. In mediaeval England, the form flowered in the hands of potters who, in good times, were supplying a lively and stimulating market.

In fact it is more likely that the spouted, handled, fired clay container for liquid foods in common use today was brought, over a long period of time, from the Middle East via Continental Europe, the shape being adapted along the way in the hands of makers who catered to the particular needs of their own society.

Porcelain wheel-thrown jug, Joanna Howells.

Jug or Pitcher – What's in a Word?

The word 'pitcher' is very old and comes from the same stem as beaker, but 'jug' appeared from nowhere in the sixteenth century, when it was used as an endearing nickname for girls called Jenny or Joan. It seems probable that it has some Scandinavian or German origin, as the German for jug is *krug*.

Tall pitcher in mediaeval style, John Leach, Muchelney Pottery, Somerset. The pitcher is wood-fired, with an unglazed exterior.

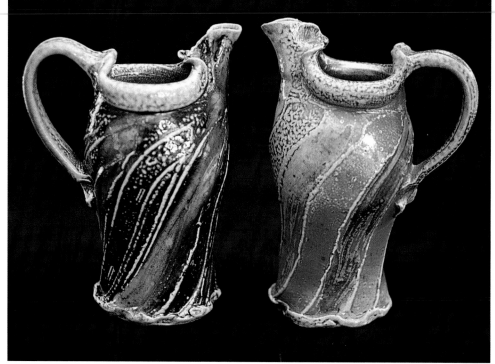

*P*air of soda-fired
jugs, Ruthanne
Tudball, Berkshire.
The jugs are
wonderfully spouted
and handled for
optimum pour.

*W*ood-fired
and slightly salted
pitcher, Svend
Bayer, Devon.
The outside is
unglazed except
by the fire, but
there is a smooth
glaze on the
inside. The
handle, with its
slight droop, fits
the form very well.

The divergence of use for the American 'pitcher' and the English 'jug' is an interesting example of language at work. 'Jug' is used in America to denote a bottle shape that is closed in at the top, made extensively in the past for various liquids, but rendered notorious by southern potters for the keeping of 'moonshine' – illicit whisky made from rye or corn.

Uses for Jugs and Pitchers

It is difficult now to imagine life without liquid containers of plastic, metal, card or glass, but before their advent, and once fired clay became serious competition for wood and tarred leather, every runny substance at some time or another came in contact with a pitcher, jug or jar. They were used for milk, buttermilk and milking, for decanting ale, mead, wine and cider, for carrying beer home from the tavern, for pissing into, for spitting into, for being sick into after surfeit, for collecting

*S*alt-fired jug with interior ash glaze, Phil Rogers, North Wales. The iron-bearing slip on the outside has been cut through before the pot dried completely.

*T*all pitcher. *Reduction fired in a gas-fuelled kiln, The exaggerated throat carries the liquid being poured in spectacular fashion. Karen Ann Wood, Kent.*

slops to be thrown out of the window and on to the street below, for using as weapons, and for cooking.

Potters in Buckley, North Wales, lidded a jug used for making jugged hare – a mixture of pieces of hare put into the pot with lemon, apples, cloves, shallots and a good glass of claret or port. In other areas a pig's bladder was pulled over to seal the pitcher and it was then put into a pot of simmering water to cook slowly. In colonial times in America a small pitcher was made for 'emptins'– for keeping a supply of yeast going from one baking to the next.

Above all, jugs and pitchers were used for water. Many of the nearly whole examples of pre-industrial jugs have been recovered from wells or stream beds, perhaps dropped by accident or cushioned by the water when thrown away as waste. Keeping a constant supply of water for kitchen

and table, for washing clothing, persons and dishes, must have been a heavy chore, even if a little pleasurable gossip was exchanged at the well or pump.

Earthenware lead-glazed jugs or pitchers were for the most part rough and crudely made, simple yet intensely functional. Those made for the table, copying designs in silver or pewter, were of better quality, displaying a desire to 'keep up', in the visual sense, with those pitchers made of more valuable materials. Despite this motivation, the nature of the material and the limited technical means at the disposal of the potters meant that a lively vitality, a sense of clay, was always in evidence.

Since life can now be led, as it was in pre-history, without the aid of fired-clay liquid-holders (though it would be the poorer for it), potters must balance the visual, tactile and useful functions of this essentially domestic form in order to make it more desirable to users than the unedifying packets and bottles that contain our staple drinks.

Fortunately there is a subconscious thread of folk memory in people – perhaps stemming from the days when every kitchen, rich or poor, sported several pitchers on shelves or on dresser hooks, and when the best of these containers were taken to table – which causes the form to be held in great affection. People love jugs and can see the sense in them. I have often been in households where the only hand-made pottery was a jug from a holiday in Devon or an earthenware wine pitcher from the sunny south.

*L*arge
hand-built jug,
Anna Lambert, West
Yorkshire. The
decoration is in
underglaze colours
with a thin clear
glaze over.

Function

By contrast with bowls, the function of the pitcher/jug is well defined. It is intended to hold, store and pour liquids. For table use, these functions should hopefully combine in a vessel that is both technically and visually balanced. Large or small, full or empty, a jug should be stable. This does not necessarily mean that only a wide base will do. Svend Bayer's pitcher has a relatively narrow base for the maximum belly width, but the form is perfectly well balanced and the handle so positioned that it adds to the feeling of stability. A neat solution to the problem of maintaining stability in a narrow form is to flare the base out to make a 'stand', as Anna Lambert has done with her hand-built jug. Early creamware or salt-glazed jugs, as glorious in their way as mediaeval ones, also used this device. Sometimes three little feet were added in imitation of silver jugs.

Making Jugs/Pitchers

A pitcher is a composite shape in that it is made up of different elements – body, handle and spout – which must be joined together. All composite pots must be 'designed', in the sense that decisions should be made before the pot is begun. Whether these decisions are intuitive or intellectual will depend on the skill and experience of the maker and on the making method.

Coiling or slabbing jugs can be immensely rewarding, though not in the economic sense! Throwing on the wheel is more usual in studios and workshops. Since the pitcher is not easily trimmed because of its spout, the thrower must be careful not to leave too much weight near the bottom of the form. However, if the spout is to be 'pulled' from the body of the pot then sufficient clay must be left for this purpose near the top. Very large jugs are often thrown in two pieces.

The process of combining hand building and throwing has become popular only in the last decade or so with the rise of the studio potter, who makes what Warren McKenzie from Minnesota calls 'non-repetitious' functional pots rather than pots from long production runs. This can allow more time for each piece. Using this method, walls are thrown and perhaps a base, then the sections are altered and rejoined to make a new shape. A possible result can be seen in Jeff Oestreich's pitcher.

Pitcher, soda-fired, Jeff Oestreich, Minnesota. The clay was thrown and the shape then altered to this oval pitcher.

Large jugs, slip-cast earthenware, Jane Cox, London. The whiteness of the base clay allows the colour to show with a particular brilliance.

Casting in a 'piece' mould is a method also used in workshops. A jug or pitcher form requires more than one plaster section. These are strapped together while the casting slip is poured, then taken apart later when the pot is nearly dry. Jugs or pitchers can be very successfully made this way, giving the potter a limit to form but great scope for decoration and glaze effects.

Handles

Once a jug is intended to hold more than about half a pint (250ml) of liquid, the handle should take an adult-sized hand fairly easily – four fingers side on. Whether the distance of the hand from the pot is then a half inch or three will depend on the balance of the design. It is well to remember that the human hand does not increase in size as the pot does, so for very large jugs or pitchers another hand hold is much more useful than a giant-sized handle. Medieval potters seemed to get the handle size just right for picking up and for tilting the larger jugs, as they would have been too heavy to pour. The Greeks, on the other hand, made great play with whopping great handles, and this gave the pots an air of grandeur and importance by swelling the volume of the form.

If at least part of the profile of a full-bellied jug/pitcher is concave then the handle design is easier, and the lifting of the jug for pouring more comfortable. A completely cylindrical jug presents plenty of options for handle size and placement, not all of them ideal for proper, easy functioning.

Pouring

*T*all pitcher, slip-
decorated earthen-
ware fired in an
electric kiln, Sophie
MacCarthy, London.
The over-sized
handle gives the jug
enormous presence.

A jug/pitcher should pour reasonably well – at least without a long dribble on to the table, cloth or floor. One way of ensuring this is to have a sharpish edge where the spout finishes. A smooth, thick spout edge will incline the liquid to roll over onto the outer surface of the pot.

Another insurance is to exaggerate the size of the spout. A triangle of applied clay, rather than a spout pulled directly on the wet jug, can sometimes make a spectacularly effective pourer, though the user made have to stand back a little from the intended receptacle.

*T*in-glazed earthenware pitcher. Terracotta body. Decorated in overglaze colours. The four little feet give the rounded form 'lift'. Posey Bacopoulos, New York.

*S*mall jug, salted, 'Anagama' or climbing-kiln fired, Janet Mansfield, New South Wales. The long firing has produced the rich colour and texture. The hint of a throat and the placement of the handle make it a pleasure to pour from (left).

*C*lose-up of jug. The white slip, casually marking out handle and form, is greenish from reduced iron oxide.

If the cutting edge of the spout is above the top edge of the pot rather than pulled down below it, the pour will usually be better.

After years of making jugs that do pour and jugs that do not, it seems to me that the complicated dynamics of the movement of liquids in confined spaces are just as important as what is done to the spout. The whole jug design has to be focused on pouring, not just the little bit where the milk or water drops out. A decent throat under the spout to make a channel is really helpful, but this is only possible or desirable with certain forms. I am sure that the small metal jugs used in many cafés that are designed to spew milk all over the table cloth would be vastly improved by being throated.

Well-made hand-crafted pottery jugs work best of all. Perhaps that is partly why they are so popular or perhaps, as a well-known maker of jugs has said, users have practised pouring until they get it right and it has nothing to do with the jug.

Group of jugs in high-fired porcelain. The soft treatment of the form with the indentations belies the extreme hardness of the fabric. Joanna Howells, Mid-Glamorgan.

7 Pots for Drinking

It is certainly true, that materials and forms affect one's enjoyment of beverages.

Robert Fournier

Changes in Pots for Drinking

*P*orcelain place setting with tenmoku *glaze, Ron Roy.*

For five centuries, from the Norman Conquest until the time of the Tudors, most people in Britain drank from wooden vessels. Some of these were humble, just a scoop of ash or holly; indeed, as late as 1803 Dorothy Wordsworth, on travels in the Highlands of Scotland, reported that drovers drank from rough bowls of wood. But some, especially those of maple burr embellished with silver, were very finely made and highly regarded. They often appear in inventories and wills, sometimes with special names that denote the particular patterning of the maple. These were called mazers after the Dutch word for maple. The verse below, from Sir Walter Scott's *The Lord of the Isles*, making reference to four famous mazers mentioned in the inventory of James III of Scotland:

> 'Bring here,' he said 'the mazers four
> My noble fathers loved of yore:
> Thrice let them circle round the board,
> The pledge fair Scotland's rights restored!'

The leather blackjack, of stitched hide lined with pitch, was a tavern favourite and is often mentioned in literature. Pubs are still called The Old Leather Bottle in celebration of the material. But in certain places and at certain times, drinking cups of clay were popular and have survived in numbers perhaps disproportionate to their use, since fired clay has a better chance of survival in damp earth than most other substances.

Mugs or tankards of whatever material remained large while ale, beer and cider or the honey-based mead and methleglen were the universal beverages. A medieval gentleman's breakfast has been described as consisting of 'a pottle of ale with a manchet loaf and a chine of beef'. Since a 'pottle' was two quarts or half a gallon, it is unlikely that he drank from anything too dainty, perhaps a tankard of the well-potted Cistercian ware that was produced until Henry VIII dissolved the monasteries.

*E*arthenware
hand-built beakers
with glazed fish
handles, Anna
Lambert, West
Yorkshire (above).

*M*ugs, Michael
Simon, Georgia. The
lightly salted
stoneware has a
glazed interior
(right).

*S*alt-glazed
stoneware mugs with
slip decoration,
Jane Hamlyn,
South Yorkshire
(opposite above).

*T*in-glazed
earthenware mugs
with sunflowers,
Linda Arbuckle,
Florida (opposite
below).

Two hundred years later, at the beginning of the eighteenth century, the equivalent gentleman would have been sipping hot chocolate from a finely made capuchine of Nottingham brown salt glaze, the chocolate enriched with egg yolks and accompanied by toast or spiced bread. The high cost of all three recently introduced beverages – tea, coffee and chocolate – and the fact that they are served hot caused the pots used to decrease in size.

Now mugs come in a smaller range of sizes, those sizes being dictated by the drinks themselves and their method of preparation rather than their cost. For example, in communities that have a close association in the culinary sense with continental Europe or the Middle East small cups or mugs are used since coffee is served thick, strong and without milk. There have been more mugs of this type made by studio potters of tableware in the last few years, which is perhaps indicative of changing habits.

S mall Japanese-style teacups, Aki Moriuchi, Middlesex. This is high-fired, reduced stoneware (above).

P orcelain mugs with celadon-style glaze, Joanna Howells, Mid-Glamorgan.

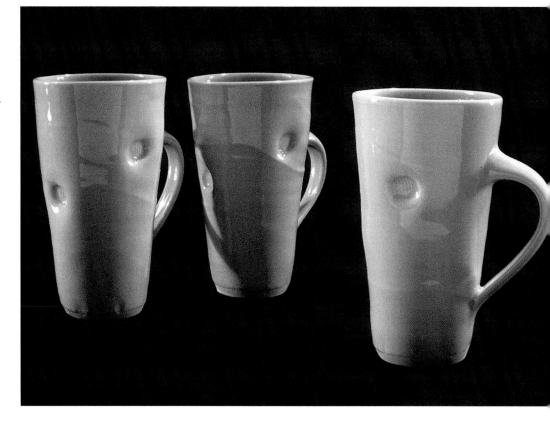

In the eighteenth century, when many new drinks, including tea, coffee, chocolate, punch and orange juice were slowly spreading while the old ones – ale, mead, possets and caudles – had not died, it was only natural that the forms of mugs varied. Now many of those shapes are the preserve of glass, whose fabric, price and durability have improved to the point where it is the accepted material for alcoholic and soft cold drinks. Mug shapes now are therefore much more uniform since they are used fairly exclusively for similar types of hot beverages. Industrial producers have taken advantage of this to put out some of the most blatantly non-designed objects ever produced by man or machine.

P all beakers for iced tea, Michael Simon, Georgia. The stoneware is slightly salted and high-fired.

T in-glazed earthenware goblets, James Burnett-Stuart. The clay for these goblets was dug from the pond outside Charleston Farmhouse, East Sussex, which was once the unofficial headquarters of the Bloomsbury set of artists who supported the Omega workshops. It is now open to the public. At the time of writing, James Burnett-Stuart is Artist-in-Residence at the farmhouse.

*W*ood-fired and
tenmoku-*glazed*
stoneware mugs,
Winchcombe
Pottery.

*T*in-glazed
earthenware with
overglaze colours,
Oliver Dawson, East
Sussex.

Only studio and workshop potters explore the form in any significant way and this surely accounts for the volume of mug sales from small producers.

Tankards are still made in some workshops, but the use of glass is so universal for alcohol that making them in clay in large numbers is probably a pointless exercise unless a market is assured. The same can probably be said of goblets, though, as always, a lively new look at these forms can often find markets where the traditional view fails.

Mugs with reduced shino glaze and cobalt decoration, Karen Ann Wood, Kent.

Soda-fired mug, May Ling Beadsmore, Derbyshire.

Making Mugs

Frank Hamer, in *The Potter's Dictionary of Materials and Techniques*, describes a mug as 'a drinking vessel for informal occasions', which it is. But there can be nothing informal about a potter's approach to making them. Mugs should be given the same care and consideration as more important works, if only because they will be used more often. People rarely buy mugs for display.

The making of a satisfactory mug is a pleasurable thing for a potter. It is, after all, the pot that gives him the greatest direct physical contact with the buyer and user. A mug or cup cannot be used sitting on the table. It has to be touched by the hand, by the lips.

The first requirement then is for a pleasant texture. The glaze on the inside has to be scrubbable because the most popular drinks today are capable of leaving behind a grungy brown deposit if not washed immediately. The rim is best turned out slightly to assist the flow of liquid to the

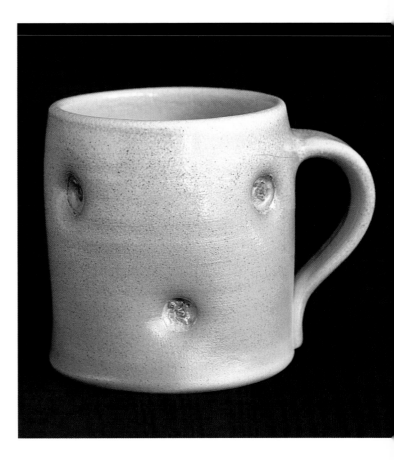

*S*toneware mugs
painted in cobalt
and iron oxides,
Andrew
McGarva, Nievre,
France.

*S*lip-cast
mugs with coloured
slip decoration
under a clear
earthenware glaze,
Jan Mair, Victoria.

mouth, though it would be foolish to make any hard and fast rules. The handle will cause a problem with the dregs if it is set too high on the form, and problems with slopping the drink over when picked up if it is too low. Both extremes disturb the balance of the picking up, and though it is possible to learn to drink from an unbalanced pot, that never adds to its desirability.

Thermal Shock Resistance

Both instant coffee and tea bags require boiling water to be poured straight from kettle to cup, so the heat resistance of mugs must now be what it used to be for teapots; these, being round, are a better shape to cope with intense heat. With the demise of the teapot to take the brunt of the heat, mugs must be frequently tested for shock resistance, and problems, should they exist, must be sorted out promptly.

Weight

The weight of a mug should always be considered along with the contents, as is the case for pitchers. Some of my favourite mugs are on the heavy side, which is fine, but it is very noticeable that no one wants to use them after about three in the afternoon, would not consider them for afternoon tea and refuse them point blank at night. They are by their weight condemned to be morning cups.

Methods

Mugs are a pleasure to throw on the potter's wheel. The rhythm of making them in quantity can be the most soothing in the world, providing they are not needed by the day after tomorrow. As an exploration of form, they can constitute the basis of a thrower's education simply because variation can be limited and function specific.

Mugs are difficult to hand build really well, so it is good to see both coiling and slabbing used as making methods by Anna Lambert and Hilary Roberts respectively. Mugs, cups and saucers can also all be cast using plaster moulds, but press-moulding is not a technique associated with drinking vessels.

The jolley technique is employed to make mugs and cups in quantity. As with bowls, a former compresses the clay, making the inside shape. A mould of the outside is at the same time revolved gently on a wheel head. The coming together of the two, guided by the potter, forms the pot.

Cups and Saucers

Cups and saucers have, since their introduction into the homes of the wealthy in the seventeenth century, been symbols of refinement and elegance. The original idea and fabric for them was as Chinese as the tea they held, but the form that the object took in the hands of the early industrial potters of the eighteenth century, such as Whieldon or

*Coffee cups,
Hilary Roberts,
West Yorkshire.
These coloured
earthenware cups
are made by hand
using textured
slabs. The interior
is glazed.*

Wedgwood, was entirely British and for a tea ritual that in no way resembled its Oriental counterpart.

Cups and saucers were never the preserve of the country workshop, except under special circumstances. Potters of 'redwares' (earthenware) in the southern United States, for example, turned their hands to making cups and saucers as well as other finer tableware when the North enforced a blockade during the Civil War. These were called 'dirt dishes'. The little bonanza came to an abrupt halt when imports of fine China resumed after the hostilities were over.

You can occasionally find examples of slipped cups and saucers from the eighteenth or nineteenth century in Britain but they are few and far between. The common man used mugs, or 'Moggs', as they were spelt in early creamware catalogues, and it is to that form that we appear to be returning. Cups and saucers are used mostly on more formal occasions and have all but disappeared from some people's lives. Nevertheless the place of the cup and saucer as cultural icon is assured by the use of the forms in the work of non-functional potters, sculptors and painters, and of its close connection with both afternoon tea and after-dinner coffee.

*Fluted porcelain
teacup and saucer,
David Leach OBE.*

Cup Shape

A teacup is normally smaller than a mug and about as wide as it is high. It should be handled generously enough to be picked up with one finger between handle and body and that not resting on the hot cup. The handle should clear the saucer edge by sufficient space to insert the teaspoon under it. The whole ensemble is much more comfortable if there is a distinct well for a footed cup to sit into. Otherwise it is free to rattle about if the user dares to move. This may have presented no problem when ladies were confined to their seats by their crinolines and men by their periwigs, but it does not make too much sense now, when only an excess of drink or ill health keeps people in one place for long.

Porcelain cups and saucers, David and Margaret Frith, North Wales. The decoration is over the glaze in a heavy iron-bearing pigment and cobalt.

Cups and saucers, Hilary Roberts, West Yorkshire. These porcelain cups are finely made from textured rolled slabs and have clear-glazed interiors.

Earthenware cup and saucer, Anna Timlett, Devon. The pieces have been coated in white slip then painted with coloured slips and oxides.

Coffee cups are traditionally taller than they are wide and, unlike teacups – which have curved sides to allow the liquid to cool – have straight sides to minimize heat loss.

The Saucer

The saucer is the direct descendant of the dish used in the Middle Ages for a dipping sauce, often highly flavoured with honey, wine and spices, which was set with a 'mess' for diners to share. The word comes from the old French *saucière*, which did and still does mean a sauce boat. Perhaps the dish underneath the handleless small cup was at first mockingly called a saucer, but the name just stuck. It could just as well have been called an under-dish; this is what happened in France, where the dish under a bowl or cup is known as a *soucoupe*.

Saucers are relatively simple forms but can be difficult to get right since they are physically and emotionally part of a pair. Saucers alone always look quite miserable.

Apart from making sure the cup fits its allotted space so it is not to be a nuisance to the user, it is important that the rise on the saucer's outer edge is at a suitable height for lifting without difficulty, since we can be certain that the liquid the cup contains will be hot.

The cup and saucer should look as though they are related by more than just the glaze that covers them. It is the idea of the two forms being related yet different, along with their cultural significance, that has made the pair so interesting.

8 Serving Dishes and Casseroles

There is a dish to hold the sea,
A brazier to contain the sun

John Davidson (1857–1909), *Imagination*

Serving Platters

Historically there have been two different approaches to the serving of meals. One involves platters and dishes piled with food being placed on the table so that diners are able to help themselves and, at least in genteel circles, their neighbours as well. The other

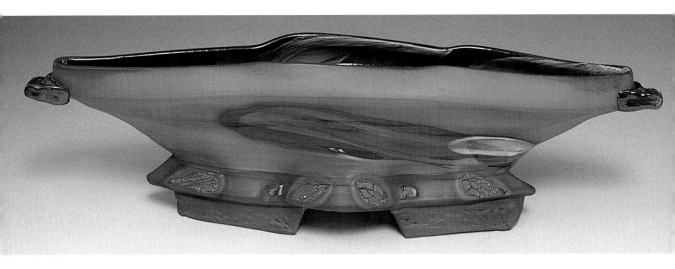

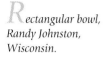

Rectangular bowl, Randy Johnston, Wisconsin.

Oval dish, Oliver Dawson, East Sussex. The dish is tin-glazed with loose painting in overglaze colours. This type of dish is formed when a 'leaf' of clay is cut from the base of the damp pot and the sides gently pushed together. The gap is then sealed and smoothed.

is where food is 'dished up' onto an individual plate, either out of sight of diners or else at a sideboard. The latter course inspires the sort of formality greatly enjoyed by Victorian society, when there were enough servants at hand to cope with both the serving of the meal and the washing-up it engendered. This is still what we expect from a European-style restaurant. The former, informal and more conducive to social intercourse, has grown under the influence of meal habits from the East, though in America, where women acquired labour-saving devices more quickly and food was always more plentiful, it has never been out of vogue.

Increasing informality everywhere has led to a mixture of serving methods for both family and festive meals, and increased the market for attractive serving dishes. The decanting of prepared foods from plastic and foil wrappings has added to the demand. The store does the cooking so all that is needed at home is a little presentation, perhaps on a dish that can safely be taken from oven or microwave to table.

*D*ish, Winchcombe Pottery, Gloucestershire. This dish is formed in the same way as the previous example (opposite below), but in high-fired stoneware.

Some Serving Dishes from the Past

The rise in the use of ovens in the eighteenth century gave a boost to dishes that could, if required, be placed on the table directly, but even earlier pots were made to fulfil a dual role even in wealthier households.

In Yorkshire and the north-east of England, where fires were always quicker than in the peat-burning south-west, batters were cooked quickly in the fat from the roasting meat in a baking dish that was a direct descendant of Lady Alice Bryene's dripping catcher pot

*R*educed
*stoneware apple pie
dish, Karen Ann
Wood, Kent.*

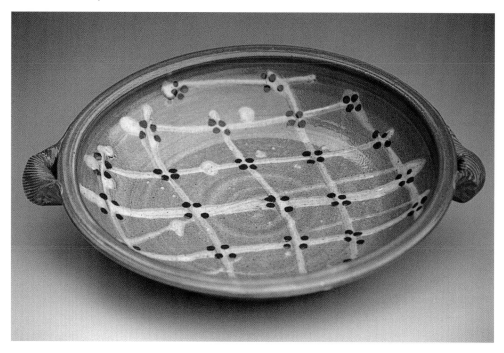

of the fifteenth century. These delectable, filling puffs of eggs, milk and flour would brook no decanting. The dish had to go immediately to table and the closer it was the better.

Elizabethan cooks had devised a 'pudding in a platter' of fruit or milk and egg mixtures flavoured with saffron, ginger or rosewater and sometimes topped or bottomed with pastry. The pie dishes that subsequently came about were even more widely used after being taken to the colonies in America. Here harvest bonanzas of apples, cherries or peaches unimaginable in Europe – where fruit and vegetables were expensive and scarce – made pie dishes a popular item from country potteries.

The British-populated areas of America produced pie dishes slip-decorated in the same way as the baking dishes of northern and eastern England, with simple scrolls or messages such as 'Shoo Fly' or 'Mince Pie', but the Pennsylvanian Dutch and German potters often decorated theirs with delightful images of everyday life sgraffitoed into slip and further coloured with oxides. Some were made to commemorate births or marriages and many bear messages or good wishes. These were to brighten mantels in the same way as the Thomas Toft dishes in Staffordshire.

Squared baking dishes, made by press-moulding, were popular products from country potteries all over. They were called loaf dishes in America since they were often used for meat loaves, an economical staple in early times, and were an art form in the right hands.

Serving dishes often reflect the cuisine of an area or time or fashion more than any other form. The char dish by Mary Wondrausch illustrates the point perfectly. Char are a small fish of the salmon family found in inland lakes and rivers. In the seventeenth century, a particular recipe became so popular that delft potters made a cylindrical dish with sides only a few inches high especially for its preparation. It was, unusually for delft, decorated with fish on the outer edge, and does not appear to have been made with a lid. Mary's char dish is a modern adaptation of an old form.

*C*har dish, Mary Wondrausch, Surrey. The white slip-coated terracotta clay is decorated with coloured slip and oxide 'char'.

*S*quare serving dish, Michael Simon, Georgia. The dish has been lightly salted and wood-fired.

Making Methods

MOULDING

A time-honoured way of making serving dishes is by press-moulding, where a flat slab of clay is lain in or over a plaster shape. This way gives a choice of ovals or squared dishes, or other non-round forms. Decorators in slip, glaze or oxides often really enjoy making moulded dishes since the unblemished surface can be used in much the same way as a canvas or piece of cloth.

THROWING AND ALTERING – A MIXTURE OF METHODS

Since there are as many shapes to be made as sorts of food to be served, potters can use as much imagination as they please by using combinations of techniques where necessary.

The two dishes by Jane Hamlyn and Posey Bacopoulos, both for oven use, are made by throwing and altering. A wall of clay is thrown on the wheel then, when it has stiffened a little, transferred to a base that has been rolled out or thrown separately. It is important that dishes that look as though food can be cooked as well as served in them, actually can do the job. If they are not going to stand the heat then another shape should be made or due warning given.

Gently curved dish with plump fish decoration, Michael Simon, Georgia (opposite, above).

Large oval platter, Sophie MacCarthy, London. This press-moulded earthenware platter is embellished with coloured slips (opposite, below).

Thrown and altered salt-glazed dish, Jane Hamlyn, South Yorkshire. A slab roller with a textured pattern has been used to roll the base of the pot, while the sides have been thrown on the wheel.

T hrown
and altered dish,
Posey Bacopoulos,
New York City. The
dish is tin-glazed
with overglaze
decoration.

SLABBING

Serving dishes can also be made successfully by slabbing, where flat, rolled-out slices of clay are cut to pattern and joined together, as are Sandy Brown's two serving dishes. One is called a lasagne dish, leaving buyer and user with no confusion as to function. Far from being restrictive, the naming of a specific function for a pot can instil confidence in buyer and user.

EXTRUDING

In cases where dishes of the slabbed variety are to be made in large numbers, an extruder – where clay is forced through a die of a required shape – is often used. This can speed up the making process, though some handwork is necessary before the pot is complete. The method is illustrated in Chapter 12.

THROWING

Thrown platters are among the very nicest pots to present food on. They have an air of making an offering, or a willingness to share about them, and since the food covers them until it is eaten, any decoration is always a bonus and a surprise. Large platters and wide dishes are not easy to throw. They require patience and attention to detail. If they are not to look mean, plenty of clay must be allowed and manoeuvred out to the rim. Platters are rarely made without turning or trimming and, in the case of wide platters, this can mean the taking away of a great deal of clay. The weight is not so important with a large platter, which is unlikely to be moved around a lot, but smaller ones should be easy to pick up, by the rise at the rims edge or by handles.

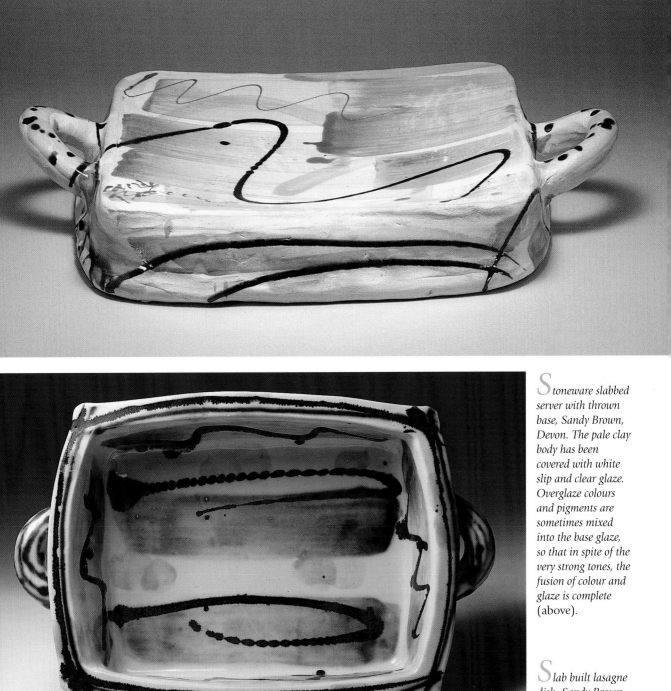

S toneware slabbed server with thrown base, Sandy Brown, Devon. The pale clay body has been covered with white slip and clear glaze. Overglaze colours and pigments are sometimes mixed into the base glaze, so that in spite of the very strong tones, the fusion of colour and glaze is complete (above).

S lab built lasagne dish, Sandy Brown, Devon. The rich brown in the decoration is manganese oxide.

Earthenware serving platter, Morgen Hall, South Wales. The terracotta-coloured clay breaks through the covering tin glaze to give the orange tones.

Stoneware lobster platter with chun and copper glazes, Oldrich Asenbryl, West Wales.

*S*alt-glazed platter, Suzy Atkins, Cantal, France.

*S*toneware platter with iron-rich tenmoku *glaze*, Ron Roy, Ontario.

Casseroles

According to *Larousse Gastronomique*:

> In the USA a casserole defines a dish made of two or more elements, the basis of
> which can be rice, any pasta, (macaroni, spaghetti etc.) in combination with meat
> or fish plus sauce or gravy, and often a variety of vegetables. This one dish can be
> prepared in advance and cooked and served in a decorative casserole. Such a dish
> is very popular in homes where there are no servants to help prepare meals.

Braise, in French, was the name given to the embers that remained in the fire to be piled
over an earthenware pot called a *daubière*. A casserole was a dish based on moulded rice,
so how the name came to take hold in the English language as the name for the pot itself
is a bit of a mystery.

Potters and others in areas where clay is readily available, that is over most of Britain,
had, according to Dorothy Hartley, wrapped food in clay to be cooked in embers, sometimes in wood-fired kilns, and the practice grew from that until stewpots with close-fit-
ting lids were widely made by coarseware potters all over the countryside. If the lid failed
to fit as well as it should then a strip of flour and water paste could fill the gap or, before
that, a close fitting stone. After all, a main characteristic of a casserole is that it is airtight,
as Alexis Soyer, a famous nineteenth-century chef said: 'in order that the aromatic flavour
arising from its contents may be imbibed by the meat or poultry and give it that succu-
lence so esteemed by epicures.'

*S*alt-glazed
casserole with cobalt
slip and textured
handles, Jane
Hamlyn, South
Yorkshire.

*E*arthenware casserole, Anne Hayter, Kent. The casserole is clear-glazed inside and covered with copper-green slip outside.

The lack of fuel and ovens during the urbanization of the industrial revolution contributed to the neglect of braising in Britain. There was no such lack in America, however, where beans baked in the same way were the natural outcome of applying the cooking method to locally available foodstuffs. The bean pots made in earthenware there exhibit a wonderful quality of purposefulness and adaptation to task and are unlike the pots made for braising in Europe.

The technique of frying the meat before putting it in the casserole came quite late to the West from the Middle East. This practice has mitigated against casseroles of stoneware

*W*ood-fired earthenware casserole, Peter and Jill Dick, Yorkshire. The glaze and clay have darkened in the prolonged firing so the fabric is fine and hard. The pot has stood up to continual use over a number of years and is still in pristine condition. The handle is particularly pleasing.

especially, since they cannot be put directly on a concentrated flame, like a gas flame. Thus the meat must be fried first in a metal pan and then transferred into the casserole for the oven. An enamelled or cast iron pot that can be used for both purposes is more efficient for the cook. But what is gained in time is lost in flavour – the clay pot is slower both to gain heat and to lose it, and is much easier to keep to a simmer rather than a full-blooded boil. This is of distinct advantage where the flavour is to be brought out as slowly as possible.

Salt-glazed casserole, Peter Starkey, South Wales. This dish was made in the 1970s and has been used weekly in winter for nearly twenty years. The domed lid allows a maximum load. The food inside is completely sealed and so needs very little liquid.

The Base

An advantage the casserole has in not having to be put near a flame is that its shape is not limited to the 'as close as possible to round' form, which is the optimum for thermal shock resistance, that is, to sudden changes in temperature. The highly porous cooking pots from the Mediterranean which are used for frying have rounded bottoms for just that reason. Even with the lifting of that restriction, other precautions have to be taken against unexpected cracks. One is that the thickness of sides and base should be as even as possible. If there is any doubt as to the clay's or the design's capacity to cope with repeated heating then a turned or trimmed base will help. If the base is not turned then the bottom can be indented slightly to distribute the heat more evenly. A thin, dead-flat base is a recipe for disaster.

Potters can play a part in ensuring durability by making sure that pots are regularly tested by being used in the intended manner, and also by including information for the buyer with the pot where it seems appropriate. If a pot is just the right size and shape for heating in a microwave oven then its suitability or not should be stated somewhere. People do not mind a limited function if they really like a pot, but they do need to know what it is!

I reproduce below sound advice from the well-produced brochure of Michael Kline's Okra Pottery in Massachusetts:

Care of Okra Pottery
Okra pots are:
Lead free
Microwave safe
Dishwasher safe
Pottery will crack if subjected to sudden changes in temperature, so it is important to heat pots evenly and gradually, never over direct flame or stove top. If you need to put very hot liquids or foods into a pot or put a pot into a preheated oven, first take the chill off by filling it with hot tap water. With proper care and attention, Okra Pottery will last a lifetime.

Salt-glazed casserole, Mark Hewitt, North Carolina. Though the potter is English, this one-gallon pot form is reminiscent of those made by early American potters for the slow baking of beans with pork fat (above).

Earthenware cockerel tureen, Anna Lambert, West Yorkshire. The tail feathers are the handle of the ladle, which sits under the lid.

*E*arthenware soup
tureen with cod
handles studded
with shells, Anna
Lambert, West
Yorkshire. The ladle
bears a gurnard
resting for extra grip.

This sort of advice is not new. A fifteenth-century recipe for a dish very like *coq au vin* calls for an eathenware pot, but warns the cook that when the pot is finally drawn from the ashes it must be placed on a bed of straw to cool: 'and when iu supposyth hit is enowgh take hit from the fyre … yf hit be a pot of erth set hit upon a wyspe of straw that hit toche not the cold grownde and when the hete is well drawn and over past take of the lydde.' (Stephen Moorhouse, *Medieval Ceramics* (1978, Volume 2)).

As with teapots, there are those who swear by the better cooking properties of earthenware over stoneware, but good design, a well-fitting lid, appropriate handles and a suitable, well-fired inner glaze are much more important than the type of pottery.

He was really more interested in telling us how good a Bernard Leach plate was to eat strawberries from with a girl he had met on board the ship bringing him home from Africa than fussing about whether the plate was turned or not. He didn't believe in fussing.

Part of a tribute to Michael Cardew written after his death
in 1983 by Michael Casson, *Ceramic Review* No 81.

T he word plate comes from the Latin *plattus* via the French *plat*. We have no Anglo-Saxon word because the 10½in (26.5cm) glazed clay disc that is ubiquitous in the Western world is the most recent addition to the range of potter's forms used for

Porcelain dinnerware, William Brouillard, Ohio.

Plate for dining in style, Sandy Brown, Devon. The stoneware plate was covered with white slip and a clear glaze, then decorated in cobalt, manganese and yellow glaze stain.

Slip-decorated earthenware plate, Peter and Jill Dick, Yorkshire.

Tin-glazed earthenware dinner plate with restrained decoration, Linda Arbuckle, Florida.

food. Before the seventeenth century, large, flattish bowls or 'messes' were shared by more than one diner, each of whom might have used their own knife or spoon, or more often, even in polite society, their fingers or hands.

The etiquette manuals used to school the children of the gentry paint a rather gruesome picture of habits to be avoided. Hair and ears should not be scratched before scooping food from the mess. Scraps should not be replaced into the dish. Hands should be frequently washed using bowls that were placed strategically on the table or brought around by stewards. Belching or nose-blowing into the mess was frowned upon.

Nevertheless sharing food is symbolic the world over, and in many countries this rather jolly method is carried out without the hygiene problems experienced by our forbears. A huge platter of delicious *mansaf*, a sort of chicken stew, is shared in Jordan, while in Ethiopia flat pancakes of bread are used to scoop a braised goat perhaps from a shared plate. Hand-washing and/or napkins then assume much more importance and bowls of water are always provided. For better or worse, French fashion and delft potters have accustomed us, however, to the individual plate.

Wood-fired stoneware dinner plate, Andrew McGarva, France.

Problems

Dinner plates are not often the favoured forms of studio potters. They require considerable space and care in drying, take up a disproportionate amount of room in the kiln and are rarely cost effective to produce. To be made on the wheel with any level of consistency they need a great deal of skill and an intimacy with and knowledge of the clay being used that may not be quite so necessary with any other shape.

Michael Cardew speaks of 'spinners', plates whose outer upward warpage causes them to spin on a central point rather than lying flat. If the central well is turned or made too thin it is likely to rise up in a nasty bulge. Rims can, in either the drying or firing, pull themselves up far enough to make a dish rather than a plate. Or they can drop if not enough clay has been used in the making.

Whether stoneware or earthenware, it is likely that dinner-sized plates will be heavier than their industrial counterparts and more likely to be criticized for being heavier, than anything else on a potter's display shelf. It is particularly hard to see this as a defect if you are aware of the pleasure to be had from a dinner plate that has a life of its own rather than the same life as all its fellows.

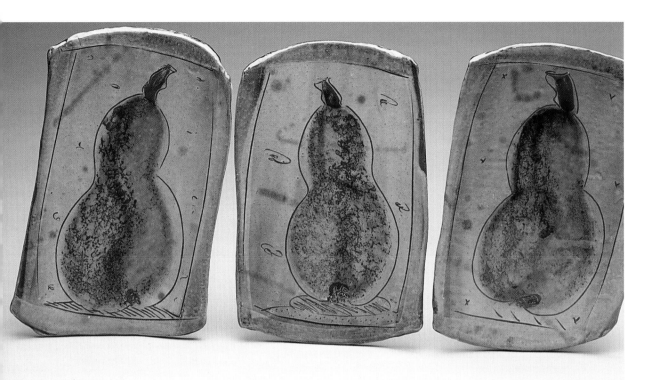

*O*nce-fired slabbed earthenware plates for fruit, Josie Walter, Derbyshire.

Thermal Shock Resistance

A basic requirement of a dinner plate is that it should be resistant to thermal shock. As a rule of thumb it should survive five minutes in a moderate oven with nothing on it, that is, just being warmed. It has to be able to do this despite being so far from the most shock-proof form, that of a sphere. Experience and frequent testing are needed to ensure that batches of plates are free from defects in materials or making that could cause that sudden loud crack in the oven that leaves the dinner plates in halves and the chef weeping.

Making Plates

Because of the basic simplicity of the form, plates can be made easily in a variety of ways. They can be slabbed, for example – cut from a rolled-out piece of clay and shaped using the simplest of tools, some foam or lengths of wood, or perhaps just lain in another plate.

Slabs can be smoothed into a plaster of Paris mould or press-moulded. A pre-shaped plaster mould is also used for jiggering. Here a Perspex or metal profile compresses a disc of clay draped over or in a mould attached to the wheel head. The plate is shaped upside-down. This last method, once used widely in industry, is increasingly appearing in work-shops and studios and can help to overcome some of the problems associated with hand-made plates, particularly that of cost-effectiveness and of creating a uniform stan-dard, for example for a dinner service.

*J*iggered dinner plate, Jane Cox, London. The cobalt slip decoration is applied using a resist technique.

The Finish

Whatever the making or firing method used, a further necessity for plates now is that they should not chip or show any sign of shivering where the clay body is exposed beneath glaze or slip. This problem was one of the causes of the demise of the delftware plates, few of which have survived with intact rims. The creamware of Wedgwood and others was much more resistant and hard in texture.

Now with the example of the absolutely non-chipping industrially produced plates it would be rare for a potter not to seek a swift solution to the problem. Glaze 'fit' is sometimes the culprit. Here the glaze is too 'tight' for the body and the tension this creates can cause pierces of fired clay and glaze to chip away for no apparent reason. Underfiring of the body so that it is barely ceramic and hence fragile can cause unexpected chipping as can some impurities in the clay where the patch of clay and glaze overlaying say, a small nodule of lime can break loose as a chip even though the pot has been well fired.

*S*ubtly shaped stoneware plates with a super-smooth tenmoku *glaze,* Ron Roy, Ontario.

Cutting Surface

The cutting surface of plates made in the West is usually large because we tend to slice up our own food, especially meat, directly. The foot or feet or base of a traditional plate should support most of the width. I enjoyed immensely making some Japanese style plates, which were just a wide, slightly bowled surface, as fine, thin and light as any customer could

Reduction-fired stoneware plates with an oatmeal ash glaze, Karen Ann Wood, London.

Square plates on small feet, Linda Christianson, Minnesota. The patterning has been left to the kiln, for pots were stacked up for firing so that each one has left its mark on the one below. The marks even show the direction of the flame. The plates were very lightly salted and wood-fired.

possibly want, and with a small footring that supported a circle of about 3½in (9cm) diameter in the middle. They were wonderful to use with chopsticks or fork foods, noodles or pasta, but impossible with meat and three vegetables. Everything had to be moved to the centre to be cut or else the diner was surprised by a disconcerting sideways tilt on to the table.

*D*essert plates, *Jeff Oestreich, Minnesota. The plates have been soda-fired in a variegated greenish black.*

Stacking

If plates are to be sold in sets they should be comfortable to stack, firstly because it is not always possible or desirable to have them all on show, and secondly because one of our habits at parties is to put out a pile of plates for diners to help themselves.

Throwing rings, the little raised burrs left by fingers on thrown plates, while admirable in some areas are usually best smoothed over in the centre of plates or dishes since it is difficult enough to scrape up peas with a fork, let alone prise them out of a furrow.

Crazing

In order to conform to modern standards of cleanliness and safety, the last requirement for a dinner plate is that its glaze be craze-free, without the network of fine lines that have become popular as decorative effect on pots which are not for use with food. Provided there is total adherence between glaze and body, crazing is not dangerous, just unsightly to some. Craze patterns on some old plates speak of the materials used and treatment

*P*retty
earthenware plate,
Anna Timlett,
Devon. The plate
has been coated with
white slip and clear
glazed, before being
decorated with
coloured slips and
oxides and fired in
an electric kiln.

*T*raditional
earthenware plate,
Huw Phillips,
Staffordshire.
The plate is richly
honey-coloured
where the glaze
is over white slip,
but dark where it
is on the clay alone.

meted out, so are part of the history of the object, but the intense heat of the water in dishwashers and the chemicals used could well accentuate craze lines and cause some lifting over time.

Forms

I had a theory years ago that the rectangular plates that slot together on a tray and are handed out at mealtimes on flights and coaches would eventually accustom a whole generation to eating from plates that were not round. It did not happen, though the theory was not bad. What has instead had an influence on plate form is the increasing interest in and availability of foods that somehow look right to our eyes on non-conformist plates. Sushi, those delectable bite-size rolls or stacks of

*B*lue eggs and ham' dinner plate, Mark Hewitt, North Carolina. The decoration on this wood-fired stoneware plate is finger-wiped circles through iron slip and blue glass yolks.

*S*et of four slabbed plates for serving something exotic, Ron Roy, Ontario. A 'soak' of the kiln at the top temperature is needed for tenmoku-glazed stoneware to achieve this surface quality – smooth and unblemished.

rolled rice, seaweed, meat, vegetables or fish are entirely at home on a rectangle or square. As in the past, it is from the outside world that habits of generations will slowly change. Many of the plate shapes shown on these pages still have a maximum cutting area, but are sufficiently interesting to show off new foods to advantage.

Plates might be a nuisance to the potter in some ways, but once made the expanse of smooth surface positively begs to have marks made on it. Quentin Bell's comments to Isabelle Anscombe, author of *Omega and After*, in July 1979 make the point perfectly: 'I tend to make things that I'm going to have fun decorating. That's one of the reasons why I make plates a lot. When I'm throwing plates I do think "Oh, this'll be a lark to decorate" – it'll be a nice field of operation, so to speak.'

Even the size of a dinner plate is right for decorating, so we must admire even more the restraint of potters who have the patience to allow glaze or fire work their magic without interference from slip trailer or brush, graving tool or stamp.

10 Teapots and Coffee Pots

Brunch is at eleven,
Punch is at three,
Coffee is at seven,
But where's my tea?

Teapots

In times before 'cha', or tea, and its pot were exported to the West, the leaf was reduced to a powder, compressed into blocks to be transported, then grated into the bowl from which it was to be drunk. This was then whisked up into a froth with boiling water – a cross between instant tea and a cappuccino. When the fashion changed to drying the tea leaves, which then had to be steeped for several minutes in water, an adaptation was made to the wine ewers already in existence.

By the sixteenth century, when the Dutch and Portuguese were bringing back to Europe small quantities of tea and the little pots to brew it in, there were many different preferences for teaware in China.

One was for porcelain, the choice of the very formal emperor and court. The whiteness, translucency and purity of the fine fabric allowed the colours of the teas to be shown off to perfection – pale amber, olive green, saffron or russet – so adding to the beauty of the ceremony that surrounded the act of tea drinking.

The choice of the intellectuals and literati was the unglazed, polished stoneware from Yixing, a pottery centre about 50 miles (80km) from Shanghai. These fine pots, which had been bought to a state of perfection over their 2,000-year history, must have been a source of wonderment to those who could afford the expensive luxury of not only the tea, but also a red or brown pot to make it in.

It was not in the least surprising that symbolism and ceremony accompanied tea and its accoutrements on the journey from the East, even though that ceremony took on a different form in the West.

*S*plendid green
'pachyderm' teapot,
Michael Kline,
Massachusetts. This
stoneware pot was
made by throwing
and altering. It was
then high-fired with
a salting at top
temperature.

*S*oftly rounded
soda-fired teapot,
Ruthanne Tudball,
Berkshire. All
possible additions
are made while the
pot is still soft from
the throwing so that
the disparate parts
have a rolled
together unity.
Coloured slips and
the fire itself create
the changes of tone.

*R*educed stoneware teapots, Suzy Atkins, France. The gold that delineates the pattern has been added after the high firing and the pots have then been 'third fired' to a lowish temperature (above).

*S*lip-decorated, tin-glazed earthenware pot, Morgen Hall, South Wales. The clay colour can be seen at the base.

*F*airly recent,
probably moulded,
red unglazed
stoneware teapot
made in the Yixing
area of China.
Many of the forms
have remained
unchanged for
centuries.

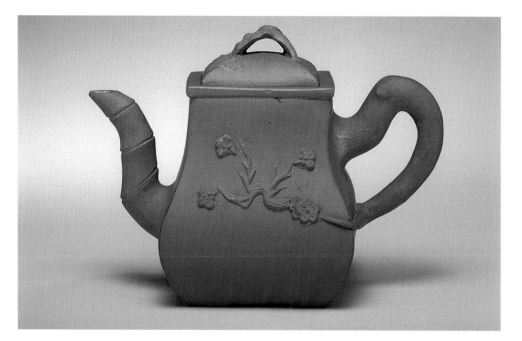

*R*ed earthenware
coffee pot, Philip
Wood, Somerset.
The interior is
coated in white slip
and a clear glaze.
The distinctive
surface comes from a
colloidal wash
applied before
the glaze firing.

Coffee

The same could be said of coffee, although that beverage came a different route, from Abyssinia by way of Turkey. The Arabs invested its making and drinking with no less ritual and social significance than that which accompanied tea drinking in the Far East. The pots they used, however, were not usually of clay but of metal.

The First Pots

At first potters in England, determinedly muscling in on what was patently a way to put their wares on the tables of the well-heeled, made the little pots for tea and coffee in the same form – a tapering cylinder with a pointed lid and a side handle. Later, as tea drinking gripped the nation, the teapot became rounder and larger, and the form developed into what has been called 'an English obsession'.

Confined only by function, supposedly (since it is impossible to imagine some of the more outlandish products actually working), the teapot has been produced in such a variety of shapes, decorations and unlikely disguises that an indiscriminate collector's life must be a nightmare.

*T*in-glazed earthenware coffee pot with cheeky spout, Linda Arbuckle, Florida.

Tea for All

The decrease in the price of tea caused by the introduction of tea plantations on the Indian subcontinent made tea a drink that could be shared by everyone in society from the highest to the lowest. The teapot in turn became a recognizable symbol of comfort, of home, of relaxed social gatherings, of satisfying solitude or equally of extravagant displays of refinement and opulence.

Coffee in America

Coffee became the preferred hot drink of the American colonists, not only because of the association of tea with intolerable tax impositions, but also because the French had very successfully set up plantations in the West Indies, from whence it became the great cash crop of Brazil. Thus it was more readily available and often cheaper than tea. Coffee became the preferred drink of most of Europe through the French and Italians, so emigrants from these countries to America reinforced the habit. A German *Kaffee Klatsch* could be just as sumptuous as a British high tea.

The invention of the metal percolator and other coffee-makers wiped out the making of clay pots in all but the poorest communities or in the politest society, where the freshly brewed coffee might be transferred from the coffee-maker to be served in expensive 'china'.

It was an Englishman living in Guatemala who effectively killed off clay coffee-pot making in Britain by inventing instant coffee, first marketed about 1909. Even so, many very satisfactory coffee pots were made here in the 1950s and 60s, when metal or electric pots were not widely available. Some were very 'country kitchen' in design, based on a lidded jug, but those made by Lucie Rie during her tableware days were characteristically elegant.

The Japanese Influence

Teapots were reinjected with a more serious air when the subdued spirituality of the Japanese tea ceremony was made more widely known by Bernard Leach, Shoji Hamada and their teachings in the 1920s and 30s. This was significant for potters, because during the Art and Crafts time from the mid-nineteenth century the Art potteries had ceased making anything as functional as a teapot, at least for commercial purposes.

The utensils used in the Japanese tea ceremony were intended to be close to nature, even crude, emphasizing the harmony that is desirable between imperfection and beauty of spirit, and giving great credence to the hand-made, the reticent, the quiet and the fitting. This attitude to the teapot was eagerly embraced by potters, and wrestling with the vagaries of its complicated yet ultimately satisfying form has become a favourite potter's sport, uniting the gravity of the Orient with the hedonism of the Occident.

There have been predictions that the teapot is not far from extinction. The obsession however, goes too deep for that. It seems a general trend that American potters are able to express their obsession with the form, while for English potters function is still the prime motivation – form and decoration follow. People still expect to use their teapots here. Unless the price marks it out as totally unusable, and sometimes even then, they will enquire, 'does it pour well?', and 'how many cups will it hold?'

*S*ubdued ash-glazed stoneware teapot and two cups, Phil Rogers, North Wales (above, left).

*S*turdy everyday teapot, Ross Michelanyon, New Zealand, 1970s. The pot has been wood-fired and the glaze is a Japanese-style shino (above).

*W*ood-fired stoneware teapot with glazed interior, John Leach, Muchelney Pottery, Somerset

The form is more likely to become obsolete in industry, with the increasing use of tea bags and instant tea. After all, a factory cannot afford to make lines that do not make their allotted profit. The studio or workshop potter, on the other hand, has long been accustomed to losing money on this time-consuming piece of tableware.

Making Teapots

According to Michael Cardew in *Pioneer Pottery*, 'however efficiently the process of making and assembling is organised, they (teapots) consume more time than most other kinds of pot and therefore are less rewarding in the economic sense.' But he follows that by, 'a potter will make more friends, and find sterner critics, through his teapots than from any of his other productions.' It is also true that the fascination of putting the disparate parts together into a whole that works aesthetically is endless, and the variety of answers to the posed problems infinite, constricted only by the desire to make the thing work.

Lids

In the first place it is important when throwing or hand building to make the lid for a teapot at the same time as the body – for some reason they never fit properly otherwise. The lid should somehow be connected in such a way that it does not drop off when the

Slip-dipped, clear-glazed painted earthenware pot, David Cleverly, Devon.

Urbane slip-decorated earthenware teapot, Sophie MacCarthy, London.

Tin-glazed earthenware teapot decorated in overglaze stains and prepared colours, Posey Bacopoulos, New York City. The feet give a lift to the plump shape.

tea is poured, certainly not immediately. A deep flange on either the underside of the lid or on the outer edge of its gallery on the pot are easy solutions, though nothing compensates for the sheer workmanship that can make a lid that really fits well.

The lid should also complete the form in a satisfactory way, even if it is going to be given a different decorative treatment. Too flat a lid, or too sunken a one on a round pot can never be disguised.

I was taught that the lid must have a hole drilled in it, otherwise the tea would never pour, and I have always put it in religiously. However, I have used several teapots from other potters without this refinement and they seem to pour perfectly well.

The Knob

The knob should be of sufficient size for the lid to be lifted and replaced without the aid of asbestos while the pot is hot. If it is too large, on the other hand, the pot usually looks unbalanced; besides, any additions that add unnecessarily to the weight of the pot are to be deplored.

Handles

The teapot's handle, like that of the pitcher, must bear the combined weight of the pot and its contents and should actually look as though it can do the job. Otherwise you end up with a nervous user. The shape of the handle must be 'fitting' for both the form and the hand. On a very large pot, as with the Clive Bowen earthenware teapot, another lug is used over the spout to give security and control when the pot is lifted. The hand should clear the body of the pot when it is full of boiling liquid. For that reason it is sometimes much more difficult to put a satisfactory handle on to a very small teapot and get the balance between pot and handle right. It is most vital that the pot be comfortable or it will never get used, never get broken, and the buyer will never need another one…

It is an interesting exercise to visualize picking up the various teapots on these pages. Even though they are two-dimensional, the mind can often decide which will be easy to raise and which unwieldy.

The Spout

Pouring is another matter. No amount of visualizing would tell a viewer that a spout will pour readily and smoothly, cutting the liquid as the pot is raised so that it does not trickle all over the place. Too many factors are involved. There are, however, a few guidelines.

The spout should taper towards the end, and the end must be level with, or better still, above the seating for the lid. Like the pouring edge of a pitcher, the end of the spout should be sharply defined, especially if the glaze is thick. The total area of the strain holes must be greater than the pouring area at the end of the spout. It is incredible just how variable the length and angle of the spout can be. There will, of course, be differences in the sort of pouring the teapot is subjected to, and this should be taken account of when in the planning stage. If an intimate tea-for-two sort of pot is envisaged then a pour that has to be conducted from a distance of four feet may well be inappropriate.

*V*ery large earthenware teapot, Clive Bowen, Devon, early 1980s. The white slip covering has been cut through in a process called 'sgraffito', which was used extensively by traditional potters in the West Country. Iron in the glaze gives the rich honey colour.

*D*etail of the front lug handle of the pot above. For a large teapot, this one is very easy to hold and pour from because the handles are so well placed.

*S oda-fired
teapot for the
adventurous,
Rebecca Harvey,
Cambridgeshire.*

S oda-fired teapot for the adventurous, Rebecca Harvey, Cambridgeshire.

The Strainer

The most common problem with teapots, especially for students, is that of the strain holes that must be drilled into place under the spout. It is a good idea to flatten that area slightly before the holes are put in, and then to shave some of the thickness away, so that the patch where the holes are to go is thinner than the rest of the body. This means that when the pot is glazed, less glaze will adhere to that patch, since it will take up less water, and so the risk of the strain holes being blocked by glaze is reduced. The holes should be cleaned out thoroughly after glaze application anyway. Many potters solve the problem by putting something over the strain holes that will resist the glaze, for example some potter's wax.

The other fault that can be very noticeable occurs when the student decides on the placement of the holes, makes them, and then for artistic reasons slightly alters the position of the spout on the pot. The holes are then partially covered by the joining of the two elements.

The Glaze

The glaze on the inner surface of a teapot must be smooth and easily cleaned, as the natural tars from the tea leave a brown film that requires scrubbing even if the user uses tea bags or herbal teas. A very matt or sugary under-fired or highly coloured glaze should not be considered. The outer surface, however, is a different matter.

Making Methods

There is a basic, easily recognizable similarity to all teapots – that is, they have a body, a lid, a spout and a handle. Otherwise the variations can be endless. Teapots can be endearing, monumental, funny, quirky, quiet, loud, satirical, suggestive. Some boast of having disparate parts by making it clear that they are joined. Others are more secretive and hide the fact, looking as though they were conceived and completed locked together naturally.

*S*team Iron teapot, Woody Hughes, New York. The earthenware pot is decorated with colloidal slips (called terra sigillata) and coloured with low-fire glazes.

*B*rooding teapot, Randy Johnston, Wisconsin.

Teapots and/or coffee-pots are great fun to hand-build from slabs or coils, but since they are uneconomic to produce unless a high price is commanded, it is unlikely that a studio or workshop seriously making tableware could afford such a time-consuming venture. However, because of the nature of the making, by far the greater part of the potter's time is spent on 'hand-building' when putting together the separate elements of the teapot whatever the making method.

*T*hrown and altered stoneware teapot with soda-fired interior, Jeff Oestreich, Minnesota.

Block moulding, as was practised by the early industrial/workshop potters, has not yet found favour in studios and workshops, though no doubt it will be revived at some time in the future.

The casting of teapots is entirely feasible, as shown by Jan Mairs' cheerful pot, but the making of the moulds for these is an art in itself.

*M*r Curly slip-cast teapot, Jan Mair, Victoria. The earthenware pot is finished with a clear glaze, coloured slips and lustres.

11 Pots for Condiments

For some reason, people have always sought to 'spice up' food by the addition of condiments, either while the food is being cooked or served separately at table. Flavours move from one place to another mostly with newcomers, sometimes with fad or fashion, and sometimes because a replacement for an existing food is superior by reason of its keeping properties, its easier or cheaper method of preparation or for its perceived health benefits. The containers that hold these accompaniments change accordingly. Salt, now thought of as a health risk in some places, is a good example.

Light lunch on soda-fired stoneware dishes, May Ling Beadsmoore.

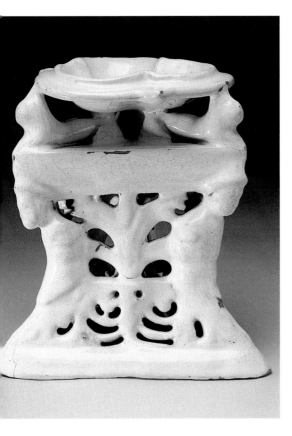

Salt

The most elaborate and lavish containers in this culture have been made for salt, not always the most expensive flavour, but in the past the most revered. Of all the condiments, it is the only one necessary for life. Severe monastic orders in mediaeval times found that salt was the one substance that could not be left out of their diet completely as they had no more austere replacement. They had no choice but to use it.

From the time of the Norman invasion the 'salt' was carried into the Great Hall of the feudal lord by a special 'cellar' steward and placed with great ceremony on the top table. These salts were mostly made of precious metals, modelled with animals or mythical figures holding aloft the bowl which contained the salt. Old manuals of manners tell us that the correct way to take salt from the cellar was with the knife, never the fingers. The great salt slowly became less and less important except at really ceremonial occasions.

Tin-glazed, low-fired, triangular standing salt, Southwark, London, c1650. This salt is nearly 6in (15cm) tall. The design is copied from contemporary metalwork. Sometimes there were small projections at the corners of the bowl on which a plate of sweetmeats was balanced at the end of a meal.

The Crown Jewels in the Tower of London contain many of these masterpieces of the smith's art, which are a far cry from the small glass or pottery shapes now in widespread use. The charming delft salt pictured is obviously part of the transition – a bit like a grand salt and a bit like the little pot in use in the eighteenth and nineteenth centuries before salt was given the additives that make it flow so that a shaker is appropriate.

The shaker is a less opulent solution and one that relies on salt flowing well, which it does not always. Earthenware is much better for the flow in a damp climate since it absorbs some of the moisture. For potters, the main problem is getting a well-indented hole at the bottom. As well as fitting properly, the cork must not protrude at all or the pot will not stand properly, but if it does not protrude enough it can never be removed. It is easier to have a cork in the top, or side. The most successful pots of this type that I have seen were cast, so that the finicky business with a stopper had to be dealt with only once.

*C*ontemporary salt with a nautical theme, David Cleverly, Devon. This salt is tin-glazed earthenware with overglaze oxides and stains. The bowl to hold the sea salt is, like the delft salt, a depression in the top.

*S*mall salt-shaker and sugar dish, Rye Pottery, East Sussex, 1950s and 60s. These terracotta pieces are tin-glazed and decorated with a 'Cottage Stripe' pattern.

Pepper

Pepper, beloved by the Romans, is an aromatic spice over which wars were fought and empires rose and fell; sadly it is better off in a grinder since keeping the peppercorns whole ensures freshness and is a guard against adulteration. Dried and ground date stones were apparently added by unscrupulous merchants until quite recent times. Pepper shakers are still sometimes found in potters showrooms but in nothing like the numbers made in the 1960s, before the Italian waiter's flamboyant flashing of a wooden or metal implement over our pasta set the trend for fresh grinding.

Wood-fired stoneware oil and vinegar cans, Linda Christianson, Minnesota.

Oil and Vinegar

Influences from the continent have made holders for oil and vinegar nearly as important on the table as salt. The Romans used both extensively. Vinegar was served on the table in one of their numerous small, flat dishes of earthenware and was used as a dip, but it is likely that it was rather weaker than modern vinegars and that it was spiced and sweetened with honey. Oil was served in a small handled flagon, not too far away in form from Linda Sikora's sprightly cruets. It seems clear that the oil and vinegar dressings we use have been around for a very long time.

Oliver Goldsmith an Anglo-Irish Irish writer, poet and playwright, wrote in the last half of the eighteenth century, of the volatile actor David Garrick:

> Our Garrick's a salad; for in him we see
> Oil, vinegar, sugar and saltiness agree.

*W*ood-fired
stoneware oil and
vinegar cans, Linda
Christianson,
Minnesota. The wire
and wood handle is
reminiscent of early
American pots.

*S*prightly Salt-fired
porcelain 'cruet' with
its own tray, Linda
Sikora, Minnesota.

Mustard

Mustard was always made into a paste ready to use in France and sold in pots of earthenware or stoneware, most of these charming enough to be used directly on the table. But in Britain the habit has been to sell the powdered form, to be made up into a paste before serving. This necessitated a small pot and these, sometimes with a spoon, have often been made by potters.

Hand-built earthenware mustard pots with spoons, decorated with oxides and glazes, Anna Lambert, West Yorkshire.

Sugar

'Sugar … is a kind of honey that collects in reeds, white like gum and brittle to the teeth; The longest pieces are the size of a filbert. It is only employed as a medicine.' Thus wrote Pliny the Elder in the first century AD.

By comparison with all of the previous flavourings, sugar is a comparative newcomer to the Western world, replacing honey as a source of sweetness for all of the reasons that a foreign food can wipe out a home-grown one. Cane sugar was easier than honey to store and transport. It also had better keeping properties and was a more effective preservative.

Double covered-jar set in salt-glazed stoneware, Steve Davis-Rosenbaum, Kentucky.

Sugar, honey or jam pot in tin-glazed buff earthenware clay, Oliver Dawson, East Sussex. The patterns have been cut through coloured slips when the pot was still damp (below).

Unfortunately there was a drawback. In the sixteenth century, when only the court could afford this new and luxurious delight, it was they who paid the penalty by suffering rotting teeth.

Sugar was at first used as a spice because it was so expensive and had to be locked away in a wooden spice chest or cupboard. It appeared in a dish on the table as a matter of course only when tea and coffee drinking had become well established as a habit.

When the price of sugar eventually fell, potters made a lidded pot for it, but by this time the porcelain and creamware makers were supplying teaware, the latter especially at competitive prices.

Sweetening the new beverages was natural since honey had sweetened many earlier drinks, though neither sugar or milk were used by the Chinese. However, their use meant that tea and coffee services were then provided with a small jug or creamer and bowl and these have been part of the potter's range ever since.

*P*ainted tin-glazed
sugar and cream
dishes on a tray,
Posey Bacopoulos,
New York City
(above).

*S*ugar and cream
dishes, Michael
Kline, Massachusetts.
The high-fired
stoneware is
decorated with a
wax-resist pattern
of vines. Salting at
top temperature
has given the clay
a lustrous sheen.

S ugar, honey or jam pot, Peter and Jill Dick, Yorkshire. The slipped terracotta clay has been fired to earthenware and painted with copper-bearing slip.

S ugar pots with spoons, Morgen Hall, South Wales. The tin-glazed earthenware is covered with blue slip decoration.

Honey

Honey has required specific containers since antiquity, when it was prized not only for the delicious flavour it could impart to sour foods but also for its medicinal value. It is likely that many of the colanders found throughout the neolithic and bronze and iron ages and right up to Tudor times were used for the straining of honey from its comb. Potters of all times have made honey pots – a good example of a form all but lost since no one with any sense would decant such messy stuff unless it was absolutely necessary.

However, contemporary potters often make lidded pots, which are interesting substitutes for the glass jars now commonly used on tables. In form there is no longer much difference between jam, sugar and honey pots. They may or may not have a gap in the lid for the spoon to protrude, and the inner surface of the pot should be smooth, but other than that, potters are free to design more imaginatively should they want since there is now nothing truly fixed about the shape.

Pickles

*Pickled vegetables, herbs, mushrooms, walnuts and flowers were
in constant use in Tudor and Stuart times. They provided ...
garnishes for meat and fish and flavouring for stews and hashes.*

(C. Anne Wilson, *Food and Drink in Britain*)

The pickles were used also on occasion to disguise bad flavours and to relieve the terrible boredom of salted and soaked meat and fish during the winter months. Our pickles today would be recognizable to, say, William Shakespeare and are a direct descendant of medieval cold sauces.

Soy sauce, an oriental pickle, actually reached Britain in the second half of the seventeenth century. It is not really common on the table here, and if it is, is served in a little bowl. Most kitchen cupboards, though, contain a bottle for the making of the more popular and easily prepared Chinese dishes – stir-fries or sweet and sour dishes. But in America, especially in cities where oriental populations are concentrated, this sauce is more likely to be served in a special bottle on the table. The form has become one of great interest to potters there – perhaps because it is now more useful in the everyday sense than that other traditionally spouted form, the teapot.

A pot to learn Mexican cooking for, Steve Davis-Rosenbaum, Kentucky. This tin-glazed earthenware triple jalapeño dip dish is for sour cream, tomato salsa and guacamole.

S oda-fired soy bottle, Ruthanne Tudball, Berkshire (above left).

S oy bottle, Dan Finnegan, Virginia. The bottle was thrown and altered, coated in crackle slip, ash-glazed and wood-fired (above right).

S alt-fired soy bottle, Phil Rogers, North Wales.

Butter

He asked water, and she gave him milk; she brought forth butter in a lordly dish.

(Judges 5, v25.)

One of the great irritations of a British traveller in Europe is that butter is not automatically put on to the table. In fact the practice is not that old here, although the practice of making and using butter certainly is. Its origins are lost in antiquity. Boxes made of wood were used by Neolithic people in Ireland when, in order to preserve butter stocks for winter, they buried it packed in salt in a peat bog. The cooper provided staved boxes for long distance transport of this staple for

Butter or cheese bells with plates of hand-built earthenware, Anna Lambert, West Yorkshire.

thousands of years. However, the coolness of fired clay made it an ideal storage container, especially when placed on a stone-cold larder floor.

In Britain, butter pots were largely coarse, unglazed and undecorated, but there are some wonderful examples of early American crocks, especially those that were salt-glazed

Butter bell and plate, Jane Cox, London. The clear-glazed earthenware is decorated with slips on white clay.

stoneware. Often they were embellished with simple motifs in cobalt and sometimes had a wooden lid that could be sealed.

The early industrial potters, after Wedgwood, manufactured every conceivable type of dish that an upwardly mobile Victorian housewife could possibly want for her table, and among them were butter dishes, at first round and lidded, to take pieces of butter that had been 'patted' with wooden paddles, or stamped. Sometimes each place setting at table was given its own little dish for butter 'curls'.

The dishes naturally changed in this century when butter began to be packaged in blocks for easier transport and sale. At Winchcombe and other country potteries, small moulded dishes were made to take the standardized block, and very convenient they were, but these butter bells by contemporary makers are eminently functional.

Cheese

But I, when I undress me
Each night, upon my knees,
Will ask the Lord to bless me,
With apple pie and cheese.

(Eugene Field, American poet and journalist, 1889)

Earthenware cheese platter, Mary Wondrausch, Surrey. The terracotta clay has been dipped in white slip and painted with oxides. The clay colour shows through as a lively orange.

Cheese has been a staple of the poor in this country for a long time, along with coarse bread and bacon. It was used especially by travellers and those working in fields too far from home to return during the day.

It is not such a necessary food now, when we have many choices of protein foodstuffs, but its popularity has never waned. One of the reasons for this is that it is the perfect accompaniment to both wine and bread.

To some extent, especially with the advent of plastic wrap, a platter is all that is required. Wood is one option but the platters pictured in the section on serving dishes would all be suitable for a selection of cheeses. Some of the most spectacular cheese dishes ever made in clay were

fashioned in the eighteenth and nineteenth centuries for the sole purpose of accommodating that most English of cheeses, the stilton, on the sideboard to be uncovered and eaten with the port after a hearty dinner. These beautifully moulded bells were reserved for the most part for genteel society, while the watered-down version, an industrially made rectangular cover and plate, did for a slab of cheddar on the tables of the less well-off. The latter are quite difficult for a studio or workshop based pottery to get right without using the casting method of making, but a thrown version of the great Stilton bell can be both handsome and utilitarian. The bell should have a hole in it somewhere to allow the cheese to breathe, and since the cheese is cut on the plate the surface should be quite smooth.

Wave form gravy-boat with mackerel ladle, Anna Lambert, West Yorkshire.

Sauces

'In England there are sixty different religions, and only one sauce.' (Attributed to Francesco Caracciolo, Neapolitan diplomat, eighteenth century.)

Caracciolo was not the first or the last to moan about English sauces. But once the mediaeval 'sawcer' had wormed its way under the teacups, at least some very nice pots were made to contain the sauces that did exist.

Delft potters made a special pot for gravy that had a compartment for hot water underneath, called an Argyll after the owner of a draughty castle who invented it. And in

*S*oda-fired sauce
pot, Ruthanne
Tudball, Berkshire.
*Just the bowl for
thick mayonnaise
made green with
fresh herbs.*

*B*eaked gravy
pitcher in
tin-glazed
earthenware, Posey
Bacopoulos, New
York City.

Staffordshire the white salt-glaze potters of the eighteenth century made some exquisite
sauce and gravy boats from block moulds, often in imitation of silver models, raised up
on three modelled feet. Some, once casting was used extensively, became ridiculously
fragile looking, and can only have been used for the most delicate of sauces. They would
be inappropriate for use in most situations today, but the sturdier versions shown here,
would all be a pleasure to use.

III

STUDIO AND WORKSHOP

*J*ohn Leach checks lids on 'greenware', Muchelney Pottery, Somerset, 1997. At this stage, before any firing, the dry clay is brittle and care must be taken with handling.

12 Potters at Work

*Although this ancient invention is well known all over the world,
there is still to be found daily something new to practise in it.*

J. J. Becher, Viennese metallurgist, from his account
of pottery making in England, 1683

T he tableware in this book has been made in the widest possible variety of settings, from revamped warehouses in squalid city streets to clearings in the middle of the wilderness, to small towns where not much happens and it is too cold in the winter, to cramped spaces in university campuses continually overrun with students. I doubt

*M*ary Wondrausch slip decorating a plate at her pottery in Surrey. The slip 'trailer' is home-made from a length of bicycle tyre inner tube.

Edward Turfrey selecting pots in the glaze room at Winchcombe in Gloucestershire. The pottery was set up by Michael Cardew in the 1920s, then taken over by Ray Finch and his family. It employs up to nine or ten people, often students and potters from abroad, such as Dan Finnegan, whose pottery is now in Virginia.

anyone could say which pots belonged to which setting every time, but potters do often seem to choose their settings to suit the sort of pots they want to make. Jane Hamlyn's Millfield Pottery is set in a landscape that is austere and strong like her pots. Certainly neither are 'prettified'. Lucie Rie was never tempted away from the city and her work celebrates the urban and sophisticated.

Space

To make tableware in any viable quantity, space is required. It cannot be done in a shoe box, however well organized, not only because it is frustrating to try to work where every surface is pot covered, but because it limits the possibility of working with other people – of taking on a student or getting hired help in times of overload, of taking a group for a short course, of having a visit from a local society or having a studio sale of work. Some of the potters featured in this book would rather jump in a bucket of glaze than take on any of these things, but running a pottery can be lonely work and those who want to stay that way all of the time are few and far between.

Some of the pots, from Winchcombe or from Highland Stoneware, come from highly sociable workshops, and others from two-person partnerships. A lone potter, in spite of the exceptions, cannot often make an economically viable unit without a workload that would make a navvy's life look like a tea party.

As well as size, there are other physical practicalities that can influence the decision as to what sort of environment is chosen. The first of these is clay, for there is more than one way of getting it into the studio clay bin.

Clay

Upon the quality of the clay depends the strength and still more the character of the pots.

(Bernard Leach, *A Potter's Book*)

The area around Stoke-on-Trent in Staffordshire was chosen as the best location for potters in the days when carting a tub of butter to market a mile away could be a day-long undertaking. Clay simply could not be transported to potters so they came to it. Although this practice might seem a little outdated, with haulage trucks plying the highways night and day, it still applies to potters keen to dig their own supply. At least there are some mechanical aids to help with this task now. Unskilled labour was often employed in the days before its advent, though it was not unskilled for long since learning about clay, where and how to dig it can be a lifetime's study. Here is Andrew McGarva's account of clay winning (given in *Ceramic Review*, Jan/Feb 1994):

> I dig my flowerpot clay in the field behind the works. A hundred years ago the place was a working brick and tile works – a tuilerie. I chose a sloping site for the clay pit, partly so that it drains easily. Also I could quickly establish a high working face, for maximum exposure to weathering and ease of digging. It comes in seams of grey and ochre, with no overburden except a turf of grass and roots. I dig it by spade into the tractor-box, take it back to the works where it is blunged down to a slip. It is sieved to take out iron stones, then run into a sun pan. I mix about three tons at a time, which dries for between three weeks and three months depending on the season. When it is throwing hardness it is lifted from the sunpan, remixed and stacked to sour a few months.

Sandy Brown in her Japanese-inspired studio in Devon. The wood-surrounded potter's wheel in the foreground is powered with the foot – a 'kick' wheel.

Souring of clay can be hurried along a little by the addition of something acidic. Phil Rogers from the Welsh-English border country adds old apple wine to his mix. Ageing is important. The longer the clay is left, the more plastic it will become. Sometimes it even develops a distinct stench, but this is all to the good. Old potters could assess a clay's readiness with a sniff.

At the other end of the spectrum, clays of various kinds and colours can be bought from manufacturers ready to use, and some potters prefer that. It is much dearer in monetary terms, but cheaper if you value your time or your back, or have not the space for a clay pit. These clays vary greatly in the quality of the materials used and in the preparation, but they have improved over the years, perhaps because of an increase in the number of demanding urban potters. With trial and error, one can usually be found to fit requirements. If not, some firms will now make up a clay specially.

In between these two, and very usual in workshops or studios with a large output, the ingredients for clay are bought in powdered form to be mixed with water in a dough mixer. This has a great advantage in quality control and in making changes or minor adjustments, something that cannot easily be done with the ready bagged stuff. It also saves on transport costs, since dry clay ingredients are very much lighter than the ready-mixed clay.

Potters have to love their clay but this is not to say that their own mix is ever exactly perfect, exactly what is wanted. It only appears to be perfect if they are suddenly forced to use someone else's, which never suits for a minute. What one clay will do without complaint another will refuse. The interaction between the potter, his working methods and his clay is one of the greatest intimacy so it is not surprising to find potters discussing the merits or drawbacks of their clay as though they were speaking of a rather capricious baby – 'Oh, yes, it likes to be fired slowly', 'No, it just doesn't like making thin rims', 'Yes, it just loves the new salt-glaze kiln.'

Clay must be well prepared for working so that the water content is evenly spread. If it is not right for the job in hand then the maker is wasting his time. This is the first lesson for students, whose anxiety to create makes them skip the most vital part. A production potter might turn out a board full of pots in a half hour, but the clay will have taken longer to prepare. A pug-mill to meld clays is part of the standard equipment of a large pottery, though often even this will not ensure that clay is ready to use without further preparation.

Making Methods

Throwing on the Wheel

Mr Bernard Leach was absolutely right when he said that there is nothing in any art quite like throwing.

Michael Cardew, *Ceramic Review,* article No. 40, 1976

Throwing pots on the wheel is the traditional way of producing tableware. And though it is by no means the only one, the physical pleasure and sense of the extraordinary nature of this activity is always shared by onlookers, whether they can throw pots themselves or not.

A competent potter can quickly produce a wide range of useful forms, plates, cups and bowls using this wonderful invention. Often people are seduced into becoming potters by its charms. It is a fact, though, that the better the potter becomes, the more challenging the skill is and the less time is spent actually doing it. A three- or four-day stint of throwing can produce a month's work finishing and firing.

Fergus Wessel throwing on an electric wheel at Winchcombe.

Turning or Trimming

Pots can be very nearly completed on the wheel head, or they may require a great deal of turning. Those who really dislike turning, which requires great patience, will avoid porcelain, since its desirable qualities are enhanced by meticulous attention to form, so that the throwing is by no means the end of the making. Earthenware or stoneware potters, on the other hand can complete an upright shape as soon as it is made.

There are many ways to work in an individual manner on the potter's wheel. Just having unique hands helps, and the restrictions of making utilitarian pots does not kill inventiveness.

Ray Finch throwing a teapot spout at Winchcombe.

Rebecca Harvey narrows a form on the wheel.

*R*ebecca Harvey
*at work: trimming
or turning a small
lid requires
concentration.*

Hand Building

A friend, on her return from a trip to Japan, was asked which was the very best pot she had seen. She replied that it was a small salt pot on a table in a noodle bar: 'Just a tiny screw of clay, as though the potter had put a tuck into a roughly cut round then folded up the sides to make a container'. To our ears this is breathtaking stuff. Pots coiled or slabbed by hand are common in the long history of British ceramics though seldom for tableware, but something so roughly constructed is, or has been, inconceivable.

The disadvantage of hand building is that labour costs are high even when proficiency is well established, so the pieces each cost the customer relatively more. It does allow more scope for personal comment, though, for wit and, in Anna Lambert's case, for a quirky quality that has more to do with the English pot tradition than the Oriental more contemplative style.

Woody Hughes describes himself as a hand builder who throws. The sequence of photographs (pp.169–172) shows what that means, as he makes one of his teapots using elements of both ways of making.

Many of the dishes and teapots in this book are made similarly, where throwing is used almost as an adjunct to the making of the pot – as a means to an end.

Press-Moulding

Press-moulding has a time-honoured role in studios and workshops. Moulds can be made of almost anything. Clay can be laid in an old plastic bowl provided some cloth is put down first to facilitate its removal. Baskets smeared with clay were possibly the first

*W*oody Hughes throwing and altering a ewer for wine (pages 169–72).

*T*he tea bowl is thrown on the wheel with thick foot (above, left).

*T*he foot is enlarged by throwing, and shaped (above).

*D*arts are taken by cutting and rejoining (left).

*T*he darts are closed to alter the form completely.

*T*he stamped spout is hand-built (below).

*T*he spout edges are closed (above, right).

*T*he spout is applied to the ewer body (right).

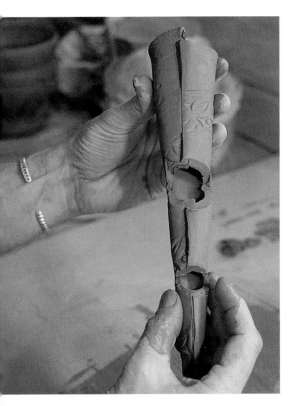

A handle is constructed in the same way as the spout (above, left).

T he holes carved in the form allow easier shaping (above).

A different handle is made from a rolled coil (left).

*T*he latter handle is applied to ewer (above).

A gusset is inserted partly to close the ewer opening (above, right).

*T*he wine ewer is completed with low-fire slips and glazes (right).

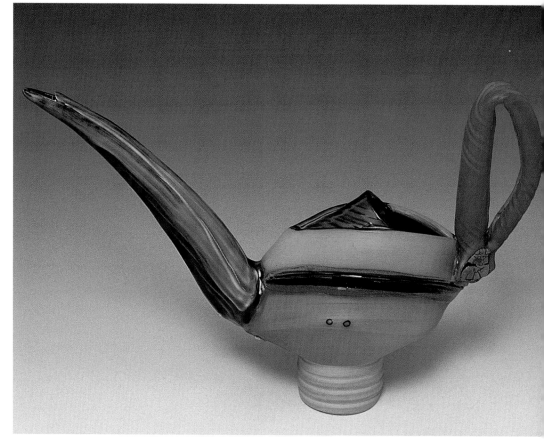

moulds to be used and still could be used today if the same precautions are taken. However, to make a run of dishes or plates in shapes not possible on the wheel – oval or gently squared, say – plaster of Paris is the perfect material.

The making of plaster moulds is an art well worth acquiring. Once the mould has been finished and dried out, a clay slab is rolled and pressed into or over it. The plaster then dries the clay, from one surface only. This gives the dish or plate a particular sort of movement that can be exaggerated on the trip through the kiln. The potential of plaster is often overlooked because it has been used in industry and is therefore considered to be incapable of making anything other than lifeless pots. This depends really where the interest of the potter lies, and what special qualities he can bring to bear on the process.

Casting

Another industrial process finding favour in workshops and studios is that of casting. With this method, a clay slip is poured into a plaster mould. A skin of drying clay forms on the plaster side of the liquid, and when this reaches the required thickness, the slip is poured off, leaving the skin.

Space is required for making and storing the moulds for this work, and as with any sort of plaster process, care must be taken that lime does not contaminate the clay. Design is all important. There is no room for changes of mind at the last minute of making, and if the pot is to be decorated as well, then this has to be taken into account from the moment of conception. This method of making is illustrated on pages 174–5.

Extrusion

Many potters now include an extruder in their battery of labour-saving devices. Although extruders have been known in Britain for a long time – indeed a 'dod-box' was used by most early industrial potters for handles – it was Minnesotan potter John Glick who popularized them by expounding their virtues on a lecture tour here in the 1980s. I remember the fervour with which potters, mostly men, set about acquiring them (or building them if they had an engineering bent).

In an extruder, clay is forced through a metal cylinder, which has a shaped die at one end. This can be used to great effect to make simple coils, or handles with interesting cross sections, or if the die has been cut to that shape, ready to put together slabs. An extruder is used in the sequence of illustrations shown here (pp.176–178) for making fish dishes.

Greenware

Whatever the making method, the pot, once completed, is called green or raw. And in this state it invariably looks splendid. Pots never look better or have a more tactile quality. It is not surprising, therefore, that this is the preferred time for decorating for some – for those potters who like to mark or carve pots, or for those who use slips, those lovely creamy mixtures of clay, water and oxide traditionally used on earthenware all over Europe.

*J*an Mair slip casting.

*T*he potter at work surrounded by rubber-banded casts.

*T*he pouring of the creamy slip to fill the mould. The different sections of the mould can be seen (below).

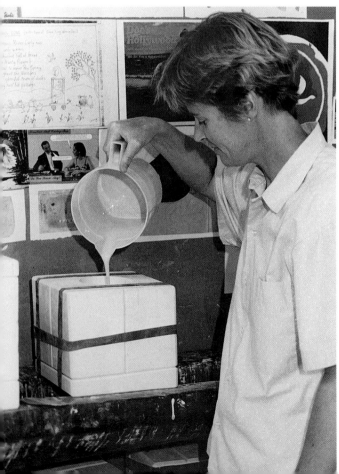

*T*he time taken for the slip wall to thicken varies, but about fifteen minutes later, the slip is poured out of the mould. If the mould is too large to lift, it has a bung-hole in the bottom for the release of the slip.

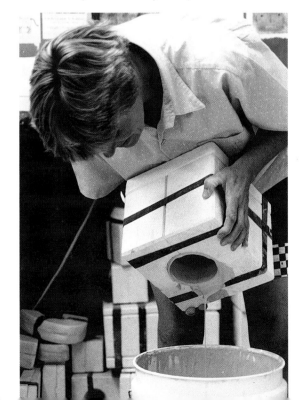

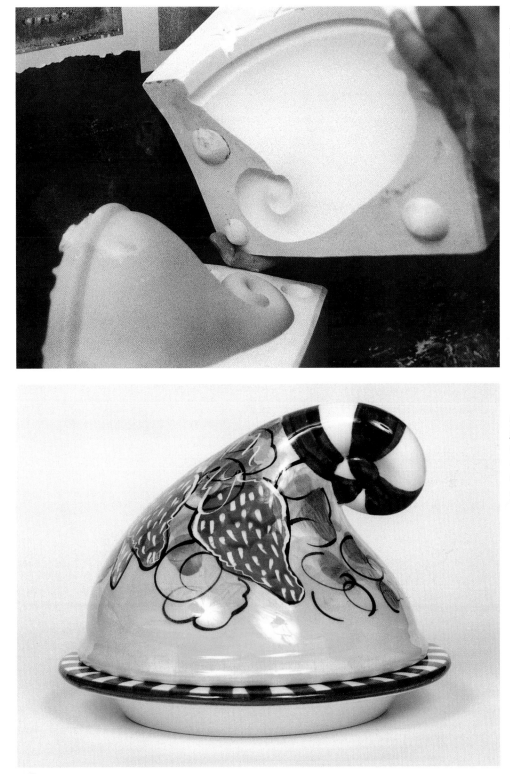

*A*fter about two hours the mould is opened to show the still damp but firm pot. Some smoothing will be necessary. The butter dish plate requires a separate mould.

*C*ompleted butter dish, 'Mr Curly', fired to 1140°C in an electric kiln and decorated with slips and oxides. Jan Mair's pottery is in Victoria, Australia.

*T*he extruder in use at Highland Pottery to make a salmon dish. Colette Thompson is the maker (pages 176–8).

*C*lay is fed through the extruder and forced out of a former to make a uniformly shaped length of clay.

A length is cut off, the tail of the fish shaped and a piece cut out so that the mouth can be narrowed.

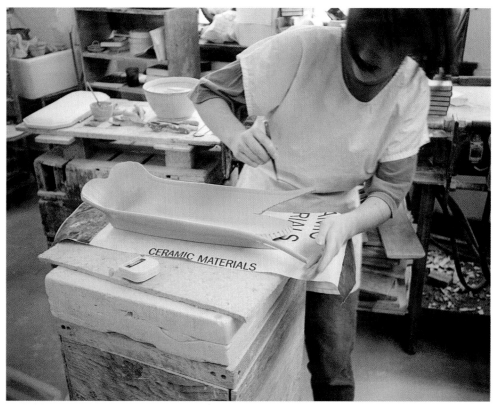

The mouth end is prepared for joining.

The end is strengthened and smoothed. For a firing to stoneware temperatures, great care must be taken with this step.

The finished, shaped dish. The runners underneath will help to spread the heat evenly as the pot goes through the firing.

Painted stoneware salmon dishes from the Highland Pottery, Sutherland, Scotland.

Firing

Raw Firing

If the pots are to be raw fired, that is to miss out on the biscuit firing and go straight into the glaze, then decorating and glazing both have to take place at the green stage. Josie Walter prefers this way. She says about raw-glazing and firing (in *Ceramic Review* No. 149):

> For me there was no choice. From the first time I plunged my arm into a bucket of raw glaze and felt that wonderful creamy texture, there was no going back to touch those hard biscuit pots which set my teeth on edge and sucked up that thin gritty glaze mixture like a sponge. I can qualify the adoption of raw glazing through economics (kiln packed and fired only once) but my attraction to raw glazing is really to do with satisfaction with materials and pace of working.

The glaze Josie refers to is one that contains a great proportion of clay so that it will shrink with the drying pots and not flake off in the kiln. The glazing of raw pots does require a deft hand, and it is difficult to accumulate a backlog of work against times of need, but it is a way of working that suits some tableware potters well, though they would be the first to admit that it has its own problems.

Other potters whose work is may be once, or raw, fired are those who work in the Eastern tradition of allowing the fire to do the decorating, or some of those who salt or soda fire.

Bisque or First Firing

It is usual to fire the bisque kiln, whatever type it is, gently to about 1,000°C to harden the raw pot. In this state it can be handled without breaking, though it is still much more brittle than the finished product. Also it is still very porous, so the body will absorb the water from a liquid glaze, leaving a skin of powder adhering to the surface.

First-time visitors are bemused by shelves of bisque and cannot quite see where these strange, ghostly pots fit into the scheme of things. They are in fact fired at a higher temperature than the neolithic peoples used for their bonfire pots and can be stored indefinitely. It was the Delft potters who introduced the habit of bisque firing into Britain, and it must have seemed a great advantage in terms of handling and painting. It also made a division

The biscuit (or bisque) kiln packed tight at Winchcombe.

Karen Ann Wood unpacks biscuited pots from a small electric kiln.

of labour much more viable since the bisqued pot could wait for the decorator rather than having to be finished and painted pretty much on the spot. The other advantage was that it reduced the number of wasters in the kiln, that is, pots that warped badly or stuck fast to those nearby. Raw pots can be stacked in the bisque literally piled to the roof providing those underneath can bear the weight.

If the bisque is fired too high, the clay will begin to become stone-like or vitrify, and then the pots will be almost impossible to glaze. If the temperature too low then they will coat too thickly in glaze. The worst problems are caused by too fast a firing. Clay undergoes the change to a ceramic material during the low temperature range, and a rapid increase at certain points will crack the pots either in the kiln or later. Any cracks are irreversible.

Glaze

Glaze materials for either earthenware or stoneware are mixed with water and stored in buckets or vats. The bisqued pot, to be kiln-ready, then has to have this powder-in-liquid applied. Depending on the desired effect and the firing method it may be that the potter needs to put an even, thin skin of glaze on, or perhaps several layers of different glaze to create a mottled or layered effect. The main ways of applying glaze are by dipping, by spraying (using a spray booth and gun) or by brushing the glaze on. If parts of the pot are to be unglazed, they can be masked off using wax or latex, or simply left. Even excluding lead, some of the materials used in the glazes are unpleasant, so strict rules of hygiene must be followed.

Glazes are almost as fickle as kilns. Some have only one thickness at which they perform properly. Some settle between dips and must be stirred constantly. Those containing ash can be abrasive and bring the potter out in a rash. One I use contains soda ash and if it is not used for a while it starts to crawl up the side of the bucket and ooze over the rim. The best behaved are those that contain a large percentage of clay.

Some types of pot are decorated either under or over the glaze layer with colouring oxides or other glaze mixtures. Examples used in this book would be pots by Sandy Brown (oxidized stoneware), Linda Arbuckle (tin-glaze earthenware) or Anna Lambert (underglaze decorated with a clear covering glaze, earthenware).

Glazes and the materials used for decorating need to be tested, tried and adjusted. A knowledge of chemistry and a little mathematics can help in the understanding of glazes, but it is not an armchair subject, but one of experience and of repeated firings, preferably in the same kiln.

Kilns

Some potters are beguiled by clay and its forming, some by glazes, some by pattern, some by painting; but for some the kiln's the thing, for it creates the final magic or the ultimate disappointment.

Electric Kilns

For evenness of firing, which can allow the potter or workshop to pursue other passions, an electric kiln is best. This does not mean for a moment that all electric kilns behave in exactly the same way, even with the latest in temperature controls. An electric kiln is fitted with lines of high-powered element down the walls and on the floor. The element control turns them on and off, so there are more off at low temperatures, more on at high. Heat is radiated in the same way as in an electric oven. In them it is possible to fire a bisque and all earthenware (but not some lustres), oxidized stoneware and porcelain.

Electric kilns are easy to use and cleaner in workshops where lots of people or students are working. They also have the great advantage that they can be left to their own devices while the workshop gets on with its own business. The drawbacks are that they are dependent on the electricity supply, that this fuel can be expensive, and that the range of glaze effects can be limiting, though anyone looking at Lucie Rie's pots, with their beautiful and subtle textures and colours, has to believe that this can be overcome, since her entire output was fired with electricity.

Solid Fuel Kilns

> *I remember one firing (wood) in about 1924 which lasted twice as long as usual –*
> *seventy-two hours. In all that time I had only two hours off and could hardly stand*
> *up at the end. It must have been during this firing that I beat a wall with my fist,*
> *saying 'why in heaven's name did I take up this maddening craft?*
>
> (Bernard Leach, *A Potter's Book*)

All of these can be used in the same way as an electric kiln, that is to do oxidized firings of earthenware, stoneware and porcelain. The difference is that in these types the air supply can be reduced so that oxygen is robbed from the glaze by the combustion to create a different sort of atmosphere that alters the appearance of both glaze and clay. Before the days of electricity and gas, when kilns were always fired with wood or coal, wares that were not to be contaminated with ash or reduction 'flashes' had to be protected from the flames by the use of saggars. These are heat-resistant boxes of strong clay into which the pots are packed. The backs of old delft plates have three little marks just under the rim where pegs jutted out from the sides of the saggar to hold the plates one over the other, but without touching.

For studio potters, the main point of firing with solid fuels is to take advantage of these vagaries. Not so much in this country, but certainly in America and Australia, some potters have taken to firing in Japanese hill-climbing, multi-chambered kilns called

*N*ick Rees stoking
the three-chambered
wood kiln at
Muchelney Pottery
in Somerset.

*L*inda
Christianson
chopping and
stacking fuel for a
wood firing at her
Minnesota pottery.

anagama. The results are sometimes patchy and there can be lots of disappointments but, at its best, wood firings can give table pots a tactile quality that makes you think that they may have just been turned out of the earth, lustrous or silky as a polished stone and coloured in the most subtle of tones, or lightly pitted and mottled with ash.

Gas kilns can be purchased from a manufacturer or designed and built by the adventurous or hard up. They use either bottled or piped gas and can be used in enclosed or built-up areas provided they have sufficient ventilation and a chimney leading out of the building. The use of salt for special effects is somewhat restricted by its smelly gas emissions. Whether these are toxic or not (and there is continuing debate on that score) they cannot be said to be neighbour-friendly, so are much better carried out in secluded surroundings.

Glaze Firing

Whatever the type of kiln, it has a box-like firing chamber where the pots – bisqued and glazed, raw and glazed or merely dry – are placed on shelves of a refractory material (the kiln furniture), which glazed surfaces must not touch.

The higher the temperature the kiln is being fired to, and the greater the space in the chamber, the more likely there are to be variations in temperature between different parts of the kiln along with differences in the distribution of salt or ash if the fuel is solid. This makes the glaze packing a matter that requires consideration, concentration and skill. A bad pack can alter the path of the flame, create cold patches or cause over-firing or insufficient reduction.

Industry has spent huge amounts of time and money to standardize kilns and firings. Wares are packed on trucks or trolleys and electronically controlled as they slowly pass through a tunnel kiln. This is necessary for continuous production of pots that look the same, but what a lot of missed excitement!

The variations in working practice among potters are as great as the variations in the kilns that can be bought or built. Some potters have a small kiln and fire it continually, some a large kiln that may take up the work of three or four months – a huge investment. Some want the kiln only to confirm and complete their work, and others require a maximum contribution by fire. All these approaches can produce tableware of note and distinction. All require experience, skill, optimism and the resolve to try again.

Selling

The cooling and unpacking of the kiln, with its attendant joys and sorrows, is by no means the end of the story. The plates, bowls and jugs set outside the kiln so that they can be better seen and exclaimed over have to go somewhere to earn the potter his living. The saddest non-selling story ever is that of the so-called 'Mad potter of Biloxi', George Ohr who, around the turn of this century became so disillusioned that he locked all of his pots, which were unsaleable at that time, in a garage and threw away the key. George's descendants worked in marketing, and when the garage was opened by them, they managed to do a very successful job of selling the lot for a great deal of money. George would have been pleased.

Another selling anecdote, this time with opposite effect, is also set in America, in North Carolina in the days of the early settlements. An excerpt from the Bethabara Church diary (quoted in Harold F. Guilland's *Early American Folk Pottery*) reads: 'Sept. the 10, 1756.

Section of the showroom at Winchcombe, Gloucestershire.

Brother Aust burned pottery today for the second time; the glazing did well, and so the great need is at last relieved. Each living room now has the ware it needs and the kitchen is furnished. There is also a set of mugs of uniform size for a love feast.' Now it is entirely probable that in this case no money changed hands, but it is a good bet that Brother Aust was a very pleased and relieved man, and that his house was full of eggs and potatoes for weeks after the successful firing. Even nowadays the people of the area, perhaps with long memories of the time of need, are invited to kiln openings, where the entire load is often sold within days or hours.

For most tableware potters in western countries, marketing is much more problematic, and probably did not feature much in their thinking when the decision to work with clay was made. For this reason, many have part-time teaching or lecturing commitments to help pay the mortgage and keep the wolf from the door. Teaching can be considered a form of patronage. It can allow potters the freedom to explore, experiment and invent without the need to produce a basic, saleable range of wares. If the teaching is done in an art or ceramics establishment it can also provide facilities for those explorations.

Patronage can also come in the form of collectors, who can be supportive not only financially but in boosting the potter's self-belief. There are times when, for one reason or another, tableware is in demand, as in the 1970s, when my first workshop sold all the mugs it could make. I imagined at the time that it was because they were good, but a glance at an old photograph is a reminder that import restrictions had a great deal more to do with it. There were simply no interesting pots about for people to buy, other than the work of potters.

Galleries and shops that have worked, sometimes for years, to build a customer base for hand-crafted ceramics are to be applauded. At best they can encourage and guide potters.

Where space and labour allow, a showroom attached to a pottery can keep potters in touch with an ever-changing marketplace and help build up local sales, which can be a great help in times of recession. There is also, ready made, a place for new work to be tested before it is set under the eagle eye of a gallery or store owner or a customer who wishes to commission work.

Part of the training for both apprentices and aspiring art school tableware potters must be the direct selling of pots. The situation hardly matters – shop, showroom or market stall. What the experience teaches is invaluable to any craftsman who is going to entrust the sales of his works to other people.

A friend tells a lovely story of his initiation by fire when he went on a selling trip with his potter boss. He was sent into a likely shop armed with a brochure and list of wholesale prices to get some orders. When he re-emerged, pleased because he had managed to get one, the boss said, 'Here lad, you'll have to do better than that or we'll starve', and promptly sent him back in again to sell more.

Why Make Tableware by Hand?

Potters from workshops once depended on making what people around them needed for daily life. Tableware potters are now selling for an entirely different reason – to satisfy their own needs and those of the users for products that not only have, but are seen to have had, contact with real eyes, real hands, real instinctive judgement, real earth. The Arts and Crafts movement of the last century, and to a great extent Bernard Leach himself, felt that in some way the dignity of men was bound up in a return to simple hand-crafted utensils and the ways of the old craftsmen. But whether people use hand-crafted pots or not has not got a lot to do with dignity. What it has got to do with is a full appreciation of the pleasures of life, of meals well cooked, of clothing well designed and cut, of sheets of cotton rather than nylon. We are in fact catering to the discerning, for those with either the education or the means or both to make choices.

Most tableware potters today mention, if they have to speak about their work, the hope that users will gain pleasure from using their pots, but James Campbell's are the words I like best. He says: 'I would like to make pots which are about enjoyment, which are loose and generous enough to be alive, and where the pleasure of the making, left behind like scent on a pillow, can communicate itself to the beholder.'

Sometimes, the good life. John Leach and his wife Lizzie fuel up for a long firing.

Bibliography

FOOD

Maggie Black, Peter Brears, Gill Corbishley, Jane Renfrew and Jennifer Stead, *A Taste of History: 10,000 Years of Food in Britain* (English Heritage/British Museum Press, 1994)

Colin Claire, *Kitchen and Table: A Bedside History of Eating in the Western World* (Abelard-Schuman, 1964)

Dorothy Hartley, *Food in England* (Abacus, 1954)

Margaret Leeming, *A History of Food from Manna to Microwave* (BBC, 1991)

Prosper Montagne, *Larousse Gastronomique* (Paul Hamlyn, 1961)

Reay Tannahill, *Food in History* (Penguin, 1958)

C. Anne Wilson, *Food and Drink in Britain* (Constable, 1973)

GENERAL HISTORY

Dame Alice de Bryene, *The Household Book: Household Accounts from September 1412 to September 1413* (British Museum, 1931)

Margaret Coatts (ed.), *Pioneers of Modern Craft* (Manchester University Press, 1997)

J. P. Kenyon (ed.), *Pepys's Diary* (BT Batsford, 1963)

Peig, *The Autobiography of Peig Sayers of the Great Blasket Island* (trans. Bryan MacMahon, Criterion Press, 1974)

Michael Parker Pearson, *Bronze Age Britain* (BT Batsford/English Heritage, 1993)

Rosemary Weinstein, *Tudor London* (Museum of London/HMSO, 1994)

HISTORY OF POTTERY

K. J. Barton, *Pottery in England from 3500BC to AD1750* (Newton Abbot, 1975)

Peter Brears, *Collector's Book of English Country Pottery* (Newton Abbot, 1974)
  English Country Pottery: Its History and Techniques (Newton Abbot, 1973)

Anthony Burton, *Josiah Wedgewood, A Biography* (Andre Deutsch, 1976)

Garth Clark, *The Potter's Art* (Phaidon, 1995)

Ian Freestone and David Gaimster (eds.), *Pottery in the Making: World Ceramic Traditions* (British Museum, 1997)

F. H. Garner and Michael Archer, *English Delftware* (Faber & Faber, 1972)

Kevin Greene, *Roman Pottery* (British Museum, 1992)

Harold F. Guilland, *Early American Folk Pottery* (Chilton Book Co., 1971)

Alison Kelly, *The Story of Wedgewood* (Faber & Faber, 1975)

Griselda Lewis, *A Collector's History of English Pottery* (London, 1969)

M. R. McCarthy and C. M. Brooks, *Pottery in Britain, AD900–1600* (British Museum, 1988)

Maureen Mellor, *Pots and People* (Ashmolean Museum, 1997)

Julia E. Poole, *English Pottery* (Fitzwilliam Museum/Cambridge University Press, 1995)

*C*andlestick with
dancers, Sandy
Brown.

Bernard Rackham and H. Read, *English Pottery: Its Development from Early Times to the End of the Eighteenth Century* (London, 1924)
L. M. Solon, *The Art of the Old English Potter* (EP Publishing, 1973)

TWENTIETH-CENTURY POTTERY
Isabelle Anscomb, *Omega and After: Bloomsbury and the Decorative Arts* (Thames & Hudson, 1981)
Jan Axel and Karen McCready, *Porcelain: Traditions and New Visions* (Watson-Guptill Publications, 1981)
John A. Bartlett, *British Ceramic Art, 1870–1940* (Schiffer Publishing, 1993)
Alan Caiger-Smith, *Pottery, People and Time* (1995)
Frances Hannah, *Ceramics: Twentieth Century Design* (EP Dutton, 1986)
Oliver Watson, *Bernard Leach, Potter and Artist* (Crafts Council, 1997)

CERAMIC TECHNIQUE
Tony Birks, *The New Potter's Companion* (Collins, 1974)
Michael Cardew, *Pioneer Pottery* (Longman, 1969)
Daphne Carnegy, *Tin-glazed Earthenware, From Maiolica, Faience and Delftware to the Contemporary* (A & C Black, 1984)
Robert Fournier, *Illustrated Dictionary of Pottery Form* (Litton Educational Publishing, Inc., 1981)
    Illustrated Dictionary of Practical Pottery (Van Nostrand Reinhold, 1977)
Neal French, *Industrial Ceramics: Tableware* (Oxford University Press, 1972)
Frank Hamer, *The Potter's Dictionary of Materials and Techniques* (Pitman, 1975)
Bernard Leach, *A Potter's Book* (Faber & Faber, 1940)

JOURNALS
Ceramic Review
Dennis Haselgrove and John Murray (eds.), 'John Dwight's Fulham Pottery 1672–1978: A Collection of Documentary Sources', *Journal of Ceramic History* No. 11, 1979
S. Moorhouse, 'Documentary Evidence for the Uses of Medieval Pottery: An Interim Statement', *Medieval Ceramics* II, pp.3–21, 1978

TALKS
Edmund de Waal and Yuko Kikuchi, 'Shoji Hamada, Master Potter', 25 April 1998, Ditchling Museum, Sussex.

Index